THE EMIGRANT'S GUIDE TO NORTH AMERICA

by Robert MacDougall
Edited by Elizabeth Thompson

NATURAL HERITAGE BOOKS

The Emigrant's Guide to North America
Robert MacDougall
Edited by Elizabeth Thompson

Natural Heritage / Natural History Inc.

Published by Natural Heritage / Natural History Inc.
(P.O. Box 95, Station O, Toronto, Ontario, M4A 2M8)

Cover Design by Marilyn Mets, Mets Studio, Toronto.
Text Production: Gringo Design
Printed and bound in Canada by Hignell Printing Limited, Winnipeg, Manitoba.

Canadian Cataloguing in Publication Data
MacDougall, Robert, 1813-1887
    The emigrants guide to North America

Translated from Gaelic.
Includes bibliographical references and index.
ISBN 1-896219-43-8

1. Ontario — Description and travel. 2. Ontario — Social conditions — 19th century. 3. Ontario — History — 1791-1841.* I. Thompson, Elizabeth Helen, 1952 - . II. Title.

FC3058.1.M32 1998   971.3'02   C98-931893-1
F1057.M32 1998

THE CANADA COUNCIL | LE CONSEIL DES ARTS
FOR THE ARTS | DU CANADA
SINCE 1957 | DEPUIS 1957

Natural Heritage / Natural History Inc. acknowledges the support received for its publishing program from the Canada Council Block Grant Program. We also acknowledge with gratitude the assistance of the Association for the Export of Canadian Books, Ottawa.

Dedication

This edition of *The Emigrant's Guide to North America* is dedicated to the memory of Clarissa Elliott Thompson, granddaughter of Peter and Margaret MacDougall, whose stories kept the memory of Robert MacDougall alive. It is also in loving memory of Robert E. Thompson, who in many ways resembled his kinsman, Robert MacDougall.

Acknowledgements

Thanks to Mary Aldwinckle, Phyllis Thompson, and Ruth Workman for funding the translation and providing advice and commentary. June Lowenthal deserves credit for the research on Robert MacDougall's life in Australia. Thanks also to the Huron County Genealogical Society for their co-operation and encouragement.

Contents

Editor's Introduction

Background

So many books were written about Canada in the nineteenth century that British enthusiasm for the subject might well be considered a mania. Prospective emigrants and armchair travellers alike revelled in the myriad details of a distant and strange land, having literally hundreds of volumes from which to choose, each one purporting to be not only true but also more accurate than its predecessors. At the same time, individual authors argued for their work's uniqueness – even though there were countless other books available on the same general topic. Some succeeded in this double task; others did not. On the one hand, consider Susanna Moodie's *Roughing It in the Bush* (1851), an extremely popular book, arguably because of its fresh approach: an account of an English gentlewoman's struggles to survive in the backwoods of Upper Canada. On the other hand, Susanna's husband, J.W.D. Moodie, failed to find a publisher for his experiences: there were already too many similar stories told from a man's point of view.

One book about Canada which can legitimately claim both veracity and novelty is Robert MacDougall's *The Emigrant's Guide to North America* (1841). Written in Gaelic, MacDougall's *Guide*, or *Ceann-Iuil an Fhir Imrich*, is true to life, drawing upon the author's personal knowledge of life in Upper Canada's Huron Tract during the 1830's: "For I was there, and I saw it." The *Guide's* primary claim to novelty stems from MacDougall's choice of Gaelic as the linguistic medium. In his Introduction, MacDougall comments that to this point, there had been no "neat portable 'guide' " designed "solely to meet the needs of the inhabitants of the Highlands." Fluently bilingual in English and Gaelic, and familiar with his subject, MacDougall proposes to fill the gap. Yet the book's unique flavour extends beyond its use of Gaelic. It is interesting to see, for example, how the author's forceful, opinionated voice shapes and changes an otherwise conventional nineteenth-century guide-book. The lively writing style — declamatory, anecdotal, referential, and imagistic — reveals him to be a man accustomed to going his own way, regardless of popular taste, an interpretation which is substantiated by available biographical information.

Gaelic in Scotland

In 1841 when *The Emigrant's Guide* appeared, Gaelic publishing in Scotland was flourishing. Earlier publications were limited in both number and scope; those few Gaelic works available tended to be religious in nature — Bibles, sermons, tracts, and so on. Throughout the nineteenth century, however, Gaelic publishing expanded to add a number of verse forms and non-religious prose; publications varied from poetry and legends taken from a long-standing oral tradition, to contemporary work, to dictionaries and grammar texts. To cite one example, Rob MacDougall's *Tam o'Shanter* (1840) features a Gaelic translation of Robert Burns' poem and MacDougall's own poetry. Periodical literature was an important part of the nineteenth-century publishing industry as well. The Reverend Doctor Norman MacLeod (1783-1862), an activist in the drive to protect and preserve the Gaelic language, published no fewer than three Gaelic magazines over a number of years; Robert MacDougall worked in the office of the third and last, *Cuairtear nan Gleann* (1840-3). Typically, the extremely popular nineteenth-century periodical literature presented a broad spectrum of topics, and MacLeod's are no exception. Among other things, *Cuairtear nan Gleann* contains emigration advice, contemporary political and social commentary, poetry, and book reviews — most notably for present purposes, a review of MacDougall's *Guide*, in September 1841.

It may seem paradoxical that, even as Gaelic publishing began to expand, the country's use of Gaelic as an everyday working language continued to decline. English gradually took over as the preferred language for trade and commerce, in the course of a natural and, arguably, unstoppable economic evolution. England was the stronger power economically, and as trade with Scotland increased, the Scots, of necessity, learned English. Moreover, English was the language of political power, by virtue of English military intervention in Scotland, especially after the failed rebellion of 1746, when all things Scottish (including the use of Gaelic) were deemed seditious and therefore rigorously suppressed. From such beginnings, starting in the towns and moving outward in ever-expanding circles, or moving northward from the border towards the Highlands and remote areas, English was heard more often, and English or Anglicized words crept into the Gaelic.

Thus, even though Gaelic was still the language most commonly spoken throughout Scotland in the early nineteenth century, many Gaels realized that the purity and longevity of their language were threatened, and that the loss of language would be concomitant with the disappearance of a large part of their national identity. Hence the flowering of Gaelic-language publications, as literate and literary (not to say wealthy) Scots launched a desperate rear-guard action against the gradual erosion and possible death of Gaelic.

Rob MacDougall was, for a short period, part of this forced flowering of Gaelic literature. After spending three years in Canada, from 1836 to 1839, he returned to Scotland and, until his emigration to Australia in 1841, worked for Norman MacLeod's *Cuairtear nan Gleann*. The heady atmosphere undoubtedly appealed to a young man who never backed down from a good argument – his obituary comments that he "held strong opinions, which in public controversy he was apt to urge with more force of language than those opposed to him liked" (*Age*), and the *Australian*

Dictionary of Biography calls him a "severe and stern" man, whose "scruples made him troublesome" at times. The result of his interaction with MacLeod was the publication of *Tam o'Shanter* and *The Emigrant's Guide*.

It is one thing to mark a successful nascence of Gaelic literature. It is quite another to determine who actually read work like MacDougall's *Guide*, or to weigh its success in stemming the strong tide of Anglicization. Instead of providing reading material for the Scottish masses, it seems much more likely that Gaelic texts were written and read by a relatively small circle of literate Scots, and, in this instance, not necessarily those for whom MacDougall's advice on emigration was designed. MacDougall acknowledges a problem when he remarks on the importance of the schoolmaster as purveyor of knowledge:

> *For, although those great and small among the people*
>> *Had enough Bibles;*
> *If they did not know how to read properly,*
>> *They would gain no knowledge from them.*

A lack of a literate populace stymied efforts to make Gaelic publishing profitable. When few are able to read, who will buy the books?

The major stumbling block was the education system. Although it is apparent that in his native Perthshire, Rob MacDougall received a more-than-adequate education, not all regions in Scotland had schools, even well into the nineteenth century. And where schools existed, students and educators alike faced another dilemma: largely for political reasons, English was the preferred medium of instruction, despite obvious problems in communication. Worse, many schools ignored Gaelic entirely, both because it was politically expedient and because there were no Gaelic texts to use. Fortunately, by the early nineteenth century, attitudes had softened somewhat; the Scots had not risen against the English recently, and educators discovered that Gaelic students learned to read English more easily if they had a basic grounding in Gaelic grammar and literature. The fluency of MacDougall's written Gaelic indicates that he was one of the lucky ones, taught in both Gaelic and English. Even so, there were still many Gaelic speakers who could neither read nor write the language, and who had no access to Gaelic texts other than, perhaps, a Gaelic Bible.

Add to the problem of literacy, the prohibitive cost of books, or, put another way, the overwhelming poverty of a large portion of the population. In early nineteenth-century Scotland, many people were out of work; others barely made a living. And in a home where there was scarcely enough money for survival, buying books was an impossibility.

Finally, then, it is difficult to assess the influence of a text like Rob MacDougall's *Guide*. Written with the best of intentions, it may never have reached a majority of the Gaelic emigrants leaving Scotland for the New World, unless information was disseminated orally by a literate, well-off owner of the book, to those less fortunate than he. Still, in a family legend, passed down from MacDougall's sister-in-law, Margaret MacDougall, to her granddaughter Clarissa Elliott, and from Cressie to her own children and grandchildren, MacDougall's relatives believe that the book was widely read and quite influential. (See the Thompson Family Papers for Clarissa Elliott Thompson's reminiscences.) Because of Gaelic literature's strong grounding in orality, no such account should be dismissed out-of-hand, even where there is no empirical evidence to support the claim.

Writing About Canada

The general interest in travel and emigrant literature that led to the publication of works like MacDougall's *Guide* is understandable when we conceptualize an earlier way of life, a time without instant global telecommunications, a time without television and computer, and a time without fast, efficient transportation methods. Most Britons of the early nineteenth century knew only the topography and social customs of their immediate locale; the greater part lived and died in the home of their forefathers. European countries were somewhat familiar, through verbal descriptions or landscape paintings, and since Europe was relatively accessible, many of the more privileged had actually visited other places. But North America was a different proposition. Few were likely to go there; fewer still could return and talk about their experiences; and writing about or sketching and painting the New World proved a formidable task. Its foreignness was the attraction for the reader; its oddities were the problem for the writer or artist. Canada contained new species of flora and fauna; its terrain and climate were novel; its peaceful admixture of races was strange to a Briton; and its social customs ranged from the odd to the outlandish. As a result, all early writers faced the same challenge – to make comprehensible the incomprehensible.

In MacDougall's *Guide*, we see some of the methods used by travellers to explain North America to those at home. For example, like many writers, MacDougall starts his narrative outside Canada: from the familiar Scottish Highlands, he takes his Gaelic readers to the port towns; he and they board an emigrant ship, cross the ocean to Canada, sail up the St. Lawrence River to Quebec, then head for the interior and an eventual settlement near Lake Huron, in Upper Canada's Huron Tract. Through this type of narrative movement, there is a gradual and logical introduction to the oddities of Upper Canada, and the surroundings become progressively more foreign in short, comprehensible stages.

A change from passive observation to active participation can be part of the narrative movement into the depths of the forest.

The writer begins as a tourist-observer and ends as a pioneer-settler. At the end of the journey, the emigrant writer no longer gazes in wonder at the spectacle about him; he lays down the pen, takes up an axe, and sets to work. This transformation is used effectively by Susanna Moodie, in *Roughing It in the Bush*, and by her sister, Catharine Parr Traill, in *The Backwoods* of Canada (1836). Both passively gaze in wonder at the sublime landscape gliding by them as they sail up the St. Lawrence River; both actively set to work immediately upon settlement. But MacDougall subverts the pattern; an irrepressible picaro, he is active from the outset. Like any picaresque hero, he sets off down the road, encountering adventures along the way. As readers, we share in the action, and as prospective emigrants, we are urged to emulate him and to trace his steps. Under his tutelage, we pack suitable clothing, fight off pickpockets on the wharf, take part in a rigorous exploration of Quebec, including a hike to the Plains of Abraham with its "not bad view." While MacDougall's insistence on activity and reader participation is not typical, it is a useful way of helping readers to "see" the strange new land.

Another strategy employed by early writers to introduce and to explain novelty to the uninitiated is analogy, as the author describes the unknown in terms of the familiar. MacDougall uses this technique extensively in his *Guide*, and people, places, and things in Canada are given a Scottish context. The hill at Quebec is "three times as high as the rock on which Edinburgh Castle is built." The skin tone of Native people, impossible to imagine for the majority of stay-at-home nineteenth-century Scots, is compared to lichen-dyed cloth, immersed in the tub three times; Natives have hair blacker than the raven, and "as rough as a piece of the shaggy hair of the gray horse;" their eyes are "like the earth berry" in colour; and the men have "backs as straight as a rod of ewe wood." To contemporary readers, especially non-Gaels, these analogies, while colourful, may have little meaning;

to MacDougall's Gaelic readers, the imagery would have been immediate and very visual.

At times, though, language and imagery are inadequate, or in extreme cases, entirely lacking. Here, MacDougall must create a new language or resort to other narrative strategies in order to communicate with his readers, as in his description of the production of maple sugar. The problem begins with the tree itself — he has no word for "sugar maple," so he tries out "sugar-tree." Then, he follows a "how-to" or recipe format, something quite common to emigrant manuals, cutting the process into a series of short, manageable, and comprehensible steps. At every possible point in the process, he inserts analogy: bring the sap to a "porridge boil," he says. At another point, analogy and language fail MacDougall completely; of the Canadian winters, he says:

> [A]ny man who has never been away from Scotland may talk, read, imagine, and dream of cold until he goes gray, but as long as he lives, he will not comprehend the extent of the cold in Canada until he himself feels it or another cold equal to it. My ears have felt it, but though they have, I have no words to describe its harshness, as in truth, the Gaelic language is not capable of describing it, and since it is not, I have given up hope that there is any other language that can.

Yet the sheer magnitude of the failure of language, is in itself a powerful descriptive tool, helping to convey the overwhelming strength of Canadian winters to a Scottish audience.

Related to the use of analogy to foster understanding is the author's inclusion of references and citations. To assist his readers, MacDougall cites passages from the Bible, common Scottish proverbs, and familiar Gaelic poems. One of his favourite poets is James MacGregor (1759-1828), an appropriate choice, since MacGregor was a Perthshire minister who had emigrated to Nova

Scotia. Many of the dozens of quotations and proverbs sprinkled throughout the book are unfamiliar to a contemporary English-speaking reader, but they would provide an instant frame of reference for a nineteenth-century Gael. Even today, they add depth to the writing — and more than a touch of whimsy.

The typical emigration manual is as much persuasive as it is descriptive. The author struggles to help his readers "see" Canada but must, at the same time, convince them that his information is correct. Accordingly, charts, tables, and maps appear in books on Canada, since such inclusions provide solid, hard, familiar details which establish the credibility of the author (who is, after all, talking about very odd things indeed), and set up an atmosphere of the familiar in the midst of descriptions of a strange new land. The Indian corn might be quite unlike anything MacDougall's readers have ever seen, but it is measured in a comfortingly familiar way. MacDougall frequently provides facts and figures, such as his chart of fares for passage to Canada, set up in Chapter Three. Later, he gives estimated yields for Canadian crops like potatoes ("forty barrels to a barrel of seed is not at all excessive"), price lists for items available in Goderich, and so on.

Other rhetorical devices serve a similar purpose. Throughout his book, MacDougall repeatedly employs the first person pronoun: "I was there, and I saw it." At times, he may cite a credible witness. Concerning wheat yield in the Goderich area, he says:

> A person may have a yield of thirty pecks to one peck of seed, but perhaps more likely ten; nevertheless, it often far exceeds any other, for I know instances when there were thirty-four and thirty-five several years. A respectable man, who was a good farmer, told me that he had forty, from time to time; and I believed him entirely.

The reliable spokesman attests to, and grounds, MacDougall's assertions.

A final component of MacDougall's persuasive prose is its declamatory style which defies argument or hesitation. The long, ringing sentences are rich with metaphor and allusion, packed with facts and valuable knowledge, alternately serious and humorous, and are meant, surely, to be read aloud. The sheer weight of detail in the long compound-complex sentences (not to mention the lengthy paragraph construction) is a part of the persuasive process, as detail is added to detail, and one example bolsters another. Even though readers may feel overwhelmed, the compounding of information is convincing.

In Chapter Twelve, MacDougall modestly says that he will give his "opinion" rather than his "advice" with regard to the best spot for settlement:

> *I say openly that I am not seeking to inculcate or force that same opinion into anyone's head or heart, only insofar as his own examination, and the validity of the reasons I present, will open up a path for him.*

But the calm assumption, slipped into the second half of the long sentence, that any intelligent, right-thinking individual will accept the "validity of the reasons" undercuts the modest opening disclaimer and comes closer to the truth. This is a man who is quite sure of himself, who knows exactly what he saw, and who fully intends to proclaim his vision to the unenlightened. And one reason for his success is the assertive, convoluted writing style.

The Emigrant's Guide provides a nineteenth-century picture of Upper Canada, a picture drawn in words by an imaginative, intelligent Gael. In his Introduction, MacDougall notes:

> *Everyone, great and small, is continually talking about the pictures he draws in his own mind — about something he has not seen, and, much worse than that, about something he has never understood.*

It is to paint a true picture and to correct any misunderstanding that Robert MacDougall has written his book about Canada, "solely to meet the needs of the inhabitants of the Highlands."

Emigration to North America

While we cannot assess with any degree of accuracy the importance of MacDougall's book in his own day – either as a Gaelic document or as a piece of emigrant literature – the work continues to offer valuable insights into the motivating forces behind nineteenth-century emigration to Canada. Looking back, we may wonder what inspired people to depart from the land of their ancestors and to travel across the ocean, in a move that was almost always irreversible. (Rob MacDougall, who returned to Scotland after three years, is one of the exceptions.) Why did Scotsmen like Robert's older brothers, Peter and John, decide to leave Scotland in 1833? And how did such emigrants choose a location in the New World? Vast areas in Canada and the United States (not to mention Australia and New Zealand) were generally understood by Europeans to be empty; despite the presence of indigenous peoples, colonizers perceived the New World, as they labelled it, to be so much blank space, waiting to be filled. Given the thousands of acres of open land, at opposite ends of the globe, how did Peter MacDougall, to cite only one example, come to purchase Lot 24, Concession 6, Goderich Township? Obviously, emigration is a complex issue, involving a jumble of reasons for and against leaving one place, mixed together with similarly diverse points for and against moving to a specific "other" place.

Reasons for leaving Scotland in the 1830's (or the forces pushing people out) might well be political in nature. The Scots had been defeated by the English at Culloden in 1746. Although this was a lifetime removed from Rob MacDougall and his contemporaries, MacDougall refers to ongoing Scottish resentment in the poem which opens his *Guide*; he pities the "careless, unfortunate creatures" who lie "defeated at the feet of the English," comparing their plight to the successful man "who emigrates in due season." Simmering or active resentment, or even political expulsion, could, therefore, be a factor pushing Scots from their homeland. As MacDougall notes, though, "it is long since 'the departure of the brave men'" made emigration a topic of serious consideration, and many emigrating Scots chose Canada (a British colony) over the United States.

Of more urgency in the 1830's was the endemic poverty of a large percentage of the population. With changing social demographics and an evolving economy, many people found themselves displaced from their traditional mode of employment, whether they were weavers in Glasgow, farmhands, or tenant farmers. A lack of social flexibility and a general scarcity of available jobs, meant that such displaced persons could not try their hand at an alternative career in Scotland. For many, emigration seemed the only solution. Forced out financially, they looked to a better future elsewhere.

At this point, the dream of improvement hit an obstacle. In his Introduction, MacDougall points out an essential paradox of emigration: those who most needed to leave were often "without the means to emigrate." A lack of money caused Scots to turn towards the New World: a lack of money prevented them from getting there.

A small amount of assistance was available – for the lucky few. There were several private sponsors, as for example, Lord Selkirk in Manitoba. Interestingly, MacDougall thinks little of this effort, referring to "the large, improper emigration that Lord Selkirk sent to the Red River." At times, the government stepped in to help, but for the most part, little aid was forthcoming:

. . . and assistance, alas! has been denied them, in spite of the utmost efforts of those who pleaded on their behalf.

The British government was never very keen on humanitarian aid. For one thing, nineteenth-century governments, in general, did not see themselves as responsible for the economic well-being of their citizens. For another, many people believed that financial assistance would lead to the loss of skilled workers through emigration, and that this would be detrimental in the future.

So if the people who most needed to emigrate were frustrated in their attempts to leave, who came to Canada? There were some who managed to scrape together at least the bare minimum amount to travel, like MacDougall's emigrant who "has not a coin with him, except to pay the passage." This man, MacDougall says, would be able to find employment immediately and could save up to buy land: "He will get work as soon as he sets foot on the land." Or he could head for the backwoods of the Huron Tract and pay for his land by working for the owners, the Canada Company:

. . . they are giving work to poor men who do not have the means to pay for land with money, but who will pay off every last farthing of it through labour.

Often, families saved enough money to send one or two family members to Canada, with the understanding that the rest would follow in due course; in the MacDougall family, Peter and John emigrated in 1832, and were followed by Robert, who arrived in 1836 with his half-sister Kitty and his father Alexander (both of whom stayed in Canada when Robert returned to Scotland).

Middle-class families emigrated as well. Even those who were fairly well off in Scotland, saw the prospect of a better life in Canada, if not for themselves, then for their children:

If the man of whom we are speaking has a family like this, it is hard-hearted of him to keep them here, as most of them will fail because of his selfishness, and it is not only to them that he does a disservice; for the children would be much more able to assist him over there than they will be here.

The MacDougalls likely belonged in this category, for Peter was wealthy enough to bring over his own cattle with him, and Robert had enough money to leave Canada after three years. Still finances were often tight at home for large middle-class families, especially when there were children to provide for, and the possibility of financial betterment through emigration to the colonies proved a powerful inducement.

Finally, curiosity and a love of adventure drew people to the New World. Explorers and travellers, like Anna Jameson (*Winter Studies and Summer Rambles* [1838]), enjoyed themselves thoroughly, whether gasping in awe at the sight of Niagara Falls, peering curiously at the Native people, or shooting the river rapids in a canoe, but these persons, by and large, were only visiting. As MacDougall points out, it is folly for someone to choose adventure as the primary motivating factor in emigration; of such a man, he says, "[M]y advice for him is to avoid it." Or at the very least, he ought to turn his gun into a "pot-hook . . . from which he can hang the potato pot."

Having decided to emigrate, whether forced out by undesirable circumstances or drawn to a dream of something better, the individual or the family must next fix upon a destination. For this, prospective emigrants relied on hearsay evidence, lectures, books, pamphlets, letters, and/or advertising literature. Advice varied – and a wise choice was likely to be a matter of luck, rather than of logical deduction, as every "expert" claimed he was right and that everyone else was wrong.

A great number of emigrants (including MacDougall) followed relatives, using letters from their loved ones in Canada for guidance. Yet letters could be innocently or deliberately misleading, as in the case of one lonely settler, Goderich Township's William Stirling, writing home in the 1830's:

> *He wrote telling them he hoped to have quite a clearing ready*
> *for seeding soon, as he had 20 or 30 "niggers" working when he*
> *stopped for the night and that the orchestra was tuning up for the*
> *nightly serenade — the "niggers" were fires set to burn down the*
> *trees, and the nightly serenade was the croaking of frogs.*
> (Thompson Family Papers)

And in this fashion, Stirling drew upon the racist, classist assumptions of his day to convince family members he had become wealthy in Canada, and, moreover, that they should join him. Although he himself followed his brothers to Upper Canada, MacDougall (who most assuredly knew about William Stirling's letters) mocks an unthinking adoption of this practice. In the guise of a disgruntled reader, he complains:

> *Useless Guide! he did not think of guiding me the way I wished*
> *to go. He scarcely mentioned* Cape Breton, *where my dear brothers*
> *are; or* Nova Scotia, *where my two beloved sisters are; or* New
> Brunswick, *where my good uncle is.*

Emigration solely for the purpose of reuniting the family is wrong, says MacDougall; rather, an emigrant ought to select the "choicest settlement."

An exaggerated form of the personal persuasion practised by settlers writing home, is the advertising propaganda of emigration agents, land companies, or anyone who stood to gain through increased emigration to Canada. Someone like Thomas Rolph, emigration agent for the Canadian government, might reasonably be expected to emphasize the good points and to play down the bad, in his lectures and his books. An examination of his writing, as for example, *A Descriptive and Statistical Account of Canada* (1841), will bear this out. Private companies, such as the Canada Company which owned the Huron Tract, were guilty of manipulation as well. On the one hand, MacDougall compliments the Canada Company on its work in Goderich Township:

> *The Company is making every effort that they can, in every way. They are cutting out roads, constructing bridges, building mills, and everything else they can, which they think will improve the area.*

On the other hand, he harshly criticizes the false advertising that had caused many to fail. Concerning Ellice Township in the Huron Tract, he says that the Company's advertising led people to believe that "this place was a little bit of unspoiled nature:"

> *The winter was warm; the summer was hot; a mill was built, land cleared, roads made, and the first harvest would be enough to pay the farmer's labour for clearing the land; he would forevermore be a gentleman, even if he lived to be as old as Methuselah; and although the world might be turned upside down, he would remain a happy man.*

The reality was quite different: the poor emigrants worked for years and gained nothing; in fact, "the poor, unfortunate people had to buy new land again from the Company, and leave the meadow as a wasteland, to serve as a lesson and warning to each emigrant who comes that way."

Even the writers who had no hidden agenda could mislead their readers. Each author wrote from a particular point of view and designed a book to meet the needs of a specific audience. Thus, Susanna Moodie, in *Roughing It in the Bush*, felt perfectly justified advising all English gentlefolk to stay away from the bush of Upper Canada. But Moodie's work would have no relevance to a poor Scottish emigrant, far removed from the social experiences of the English middle class. As a knowledgable, practical farmer (and loyal Scot), MacDougall often criticizes the advice of "English" writers. Concerning grass (hay), he says:

> [D]o not promise yourself that you will have five or six Tons an acre, as some of the English Writers maintain: two Tons an acre is not a bad crop in that part of the world.

The key to successful emigration, in other words, is to find a writer whose background and experience most perfectly matches the emigrant's own, and one who is disinterested, practical, and accurate. MacDougall insists that his work is invaluable to a Gael: he writes in a "language which has no need of a translator"; he marks out the "rocks, on which he almost was, and on which many other men were shipwrecked"; and he writes from a humanitarian desire to help his fellow Scots.

Conclusion

Except for brief mentions by a few historians, MacDougall's *Guide* has virtually disappeared from view; there are few extant copies, as for example, the one in the British museum library. Even photocopies are scarce and special permission is required to obtain one. This is a pity, for the work merits close reading. It is a Scottish document, an essential part of a long-standing tradition of Gaelic publishing; it is a Canadian document, describing the newly-settled Huron Tract of 1836 to 1839, and offering candid comments on the practices of the Canada Company; it is emigrant literature, situated within a large body of work about pioneer Canada; and, leaving the serious analysis aside, it is sheer fun to read, getting to know the book's well-read, opinionated, and fascinating author through his discursive, anecdotal writing.

On This Edition of the Text

This edition of *The Emigrant's Guide to North America* has been taken from David Livingston-Lowe's able translation of the work (1997), commissioned specifically for this publication through MacDougall descendants. Because this is a nineteenth-century document, reflecting nineteenth-century political, literary, and social sensibilities, however, the following editing changes have been made to the original translation. Sentence and paragraph structure have been restored as much as possible to reflect the original Gaelic text of 1841, with its long sentences and weighty paragraphs. Italics, parentheses, dashes, quotation marks, capital letters, and other punctuation marks and textual notations, have been put back into the text. It is important to see where MacDougall placed emphasis, even when his use of punctuation and type face seems inconsistent. Diction has been revised at awkward points, with an eye to removing confusion and to restoring the musicality of the original Gaelic. Contemporary expressions produced in this late 20th century translation, have been removed wherever possible, and although, at times, the nineteenth-century terminology may seem offensive to today's readers it is valuable to recognize the attitudes and mores of the time. Footnotes are kept to a bare minimum. The resulting text comes as close as possible in appearance and tone to the original, as designed and written by Robert MacDougall, Esq.

Elizabeth Thompson

MacDougall/McDougall Family Tree

A McDougall family from Argyll was invited, by a Stewart relative, to take up residence in the Fortingall area of Perthshire. They came and encouraged other members of the clan to join them. By the 18th century there were members of the McDougall clan living in the area. From Parish of Fortingall records:

FIRST MARRIAGE:

*Alexander MacDougall = m. (1798) = Girsel (Grace) Stewart
(b.? - d. 1836)*

— Peter (ch. 1799 - d. 1850) = m. (ca. 1831) Margaret Stewart
      To Goderich Township in Huron Tract in 1833
— William (ch. 1801)
— Alexander (ch. 1802)
— John (ch. 1805 - d. 1885) = m. (1843) = Anne (Nancy)
      Chisholm
      To Goderich Township in Huron Tract in 1833
— Donald (ch. 1807)
— Archibald (ch. 1809) - m. (1838) = Sibyla McLean Shire(?)
      Kirkton
— Anne (ch. 1811) = m. (1832) = John Campbell
— Robert (b. 1813 - d. 1887) = m. = Margaret Rankin of
      Tasmania

SECOND MARRIAGE:

Alexander MacDougall = m. (1819) = (2) Christian Menzies

—Hugh (ch. 1820)
—Katherine (Kitty) (ch. 1821 - d. 1908)
    Came to Upper Canada in 1836. Not married.

PETER MACDOUGALL — FIRST BORN SON OF ALEXANDER

Alexander MacDougall = m. (1798) (1) Girsel (Grace) Stewart
(b.? - d. 1836)

Peter = married (ca. 1831 = Margaret Stewart (first cousin)
(ch. 1799 - d. 1850)

— Alexander (b. 1833 in Scotland? on board ship? d. 1890's)
    Not married.
— William Stewart (b. in UC 1835 - d. 1936)
    - Married = Lizzie Anderson
    - Four children: William, Mary Helen (Nell),
     Margaret, Jessie
— Hannah (b. in Upper Canada 1837 - d. 1907.) Not married.
  Grace (b. in Upper Canada 1839 - d?) = m. James Warrener
    and went to Oakland, Calif.

- Two sons: William, Stewart

— Richmond (b. in Upper Canada 1839) = m. (1) Frank Murray
    - Two children: Frank, Margaret
    - m. (2) William Bannister
    - Two children: Maud, Nina: Stepchild: Lillian

— Ann (b. 1843 - d. 1900 = m = William Elliott
    - Seven children: Isadore, Jack, William, Victor, Thomas,
      Clarrissa (Cress), Benson

— Helen (b. 1846 - d. 1917) = m. = James MacDonald
    - Eight children: Peter, Florence, James, Glengarry,
      William, Frank, Colin, Alda

— Donald Stewart (b. 1848 - d. 1916) = m = Mary Ann Morgan
    - Ten children: Maud, Mowat, Roy, Douglas, Wm
      (Scotty), N. Gordon, Gladys, Wallace (Jake), Bruce, Jessie

— Peter (b. 1850 - d. 1917). Not married.

Peter and Margaret MacDougall came and settled in Goderich Township in the Huron Tract in 1833.

JOHN MACDOUGALL - FOURTH SON OF ALEXANDER

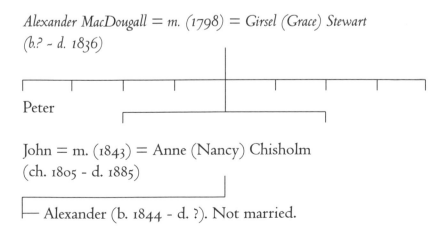

Alexander MacDougall = m. (1798) = Girsel (Grace) Stewart
(b.? - d. 1836)

Peter

John = m. (1843) = Anne (Nancy) Chisholm
(ch. 1805 - d. 1885)

— Alexander (b. 1844 - d. ?). Not married.

— Archibald (b. 1846 - d. ?) = m. = Isabella Sterling
    - Two children: Grace, John Norman
— John (b. 1848 - d. ?) = m. = Mary Corrigan
    - Five children: Annie, Catherine (Kate), Wm A.
     (Chippy), Christena, Austin
— Grace M. (b. 1851 - d. 1834) = m. = Tom McDonald
    - Two children: John Duncan, Wm. Angus
— Annie (B. 1854 - d. 1925). Not married.
— Margaret (b. 1857 - d. 1941) = m. = Wm Stirling
    - Five children in North Dakota: Anne, Ruby,
     Catharine, John, William. Margaret and children
     returned to Goderich Twp. after William's death.
— Catherine (Kate) (b. 1859 - d. 1942). Not married.
— Peter (b. 1863 - d. 1942) = m. = Jessie Stirling
    - Two children: Murray, Marian

John left Scotland with his brother Peter and arrived in Goderich Township, Huron Tract, in 1833.

ROBERT MACDOUGALL - YOUNGEST SON OF ALEXANDER'S FIRST MARRIAGE.

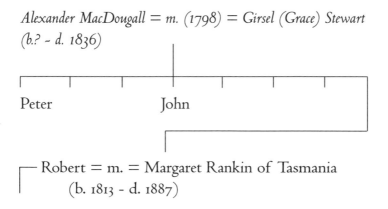

Alexander MacDougall = m. (1798) = Girsel (Grace) Stewart (b.? - d. 1836)

Peter   John

— Robert = m. = Margaret Rankin of Tasmania
    (b. 1813 - d. 1887)

— Caroline (b. 1854 - d. 1942) = m. = A. Cameron
— Jane (b. ca. 1856) = m. = Alexander Smith
  - Two children: Robert (Robin) McDougall (ca. 1892 - 1952), Heather (d. 1957). Neither married..
— Alexander (Alister) (b. ca. 1858) = m. (1888) = Janet (Jessie) Forrester
  - Four children: Keith Allister (b. 1893), Archibald William (1895 - 1996), Robert Charles (b. 1899), Mildred (d. 1950)
— Margaret (b. 1860 - d. 1935) = m. (1899) = Robert Dodd
— Grace (b. 1862 - d. 1940). Not married.
— Ann Helena (b. 1872 - d. 1950). Not married.

Robert McDougall, author of *The Emigrant's Guide to North America* came to Upper Canada to Goderich Township in the Huron Tract in 1836, along with his father, Alexander, and his stepsister, Kitty. They joined Peter and John who had emigrated three years earlier. Robert stayed for three years, returned to Scotland and ultimately settled in Australia in 1842.

Genealogical Charts — source material courtesy of Mrs. Phyllis Thompson of Clinton, Ontario.

CEANN-IÙIL AN FHIR-IMRICH DO DH'AMERICA MU-THUATH;

OR,

THE EMIGRANT'S GUIDE TO NORTH AMERICA.

By ROBERT M'DOUGALL, Esq.

Ni fear a dh'fhalbhas 'na thràth
  Biadh 'us bàrr 'sam bi toirt ;
Am feadh bhios tàchrain gun stàth,
  A' dol bàs leis a ghort :
Bithidh piseach agus loinn
  Air a chloinn 's air a mhnaoidh ;
Am feadh bhios truaghain gun agoinn,
  Fo na Goill air an claoidh.

GLASGOW:
J. & P. CAMPBELL, 24, GLASSFORD STREET.
OBAN: J. MILLER.—INVERNESS: J. BAIN & CO.
DINGWALL: A. KEITH.

MDCCCXLI.

TO THE EMIGRANT

When a skipper sets his ship under sail in his native harbour, many an eye beholds him. Some will say, privately, to their companions, – "Don't you think he will do well;" but others, at the same time, will say, – "Mischief take him! he's not worth a piece of eight; I won't believe in his success, until I know he is past the promontory:" however, no one should say that to the skipper in public. He will release the ship, and set its keel for the face of the gulf. If he has the advantage of calm winds, he will set each sail according to its purpose; if it becomes rough overhead, he will kilt up the sail's folds, and he will stay the course as best as he can. When the tempest is greatest, and the danger is closest, he has only to say the word, and his mates will stand beside each tackle, and at the end of each yardarm, as experienced, and almost as wise, as the squirrels in the nut grove around Hallow-tide. Finally, the skipper will be near his chosen destination; but, alas! he does not know the right channel into the harbour. There is turbulent water over hidden rocks on the windward shore, and flame-topped foam laughing on the lee shore. Behold his heart's agony! do the bitter words of his mouth, and the restless rage of his eyes, not adequately express his fear? While he is very anxious over what may be in store for him, who appears but a formal guide, with his agile little fishing boat, and in the twinkling of an eye, he is on the upper deck of the ship. "Let out the folds of the main-sail," he says, "and give her more speed." "Stop, stop, foolhardy man," says the skipper; "shall I place myself and my crew in danger of drowning, my vessel and its cargo in danger of loss, on your account, you impudent fellow? Show me your proof that you have studied to be a guide!" The guide thrusts his hand into his pocket; he takes out his written authority, and waves it under the skipper's nose; and not another word, good or bad, will come out of the skipper's mouth.

Is all of this not like the Emigrant's situation? He was minding his own business at home, carrying on as he saw fit; he knew what he was about, and he had no need of anyone's advice. Now he is seeking the shore of a land which he does not know; the "Guide" is a full set of sails, that will steer the emigrant to the desired harbour; and a letter of commission is stretched out before him, written in a language which has no need of a translator. Let the emigrant come under his protection, let him depend on him, he is loyal to his own; for there is not a drop in his veins except the best Gaelic blood. But before setting off, the "Guide" would like to present one complaint – that is, how grieved he is that he had to leave many a sunken rock and remote skerry off his map, because of the great haste he made to write it, and especially because of how small it is. Nevertheless, those rocks, on which he almost was, and on which many other men were shipwrecked, are clearly marked out. May the Emigrant not doubt the truth, I pray of him; for no man put a word here, but

His gentle friend,

And ever true,

ROB MACDOUGALL

INTRODUCTION

The emigration of the Gaels to North America has become the subject of much talk, not only for the inhabitants of "the Glens" (for it is long since the day "the departure of the brave men" caused them to talk about this matter), but also for the rulers of the land; even the high council of the kingdom considered it worthy of their own close examination recently. This raised the interest of the entire population so that everyone, young and old, was waiting diligently for "the bounty at the end of the tale." But this awakening of interest only served to remind them that

> "The old woman's grip is more powerful
> Than the pull of the warrior."

The Gaels are left as they were before — many of them without the means to emigrate; and assistance, alas! has been denied them, in spite of the utmost efforts of those who pleaded on their behalf. But although this put a stop to their emigration in large numbers, it did not silence their mouths from speaking about emigration; America is as fresh a story as it ever was. Everyone, great and small, is continually talking about the pictures he draws in his own mind — about something he has not seen, and, much worse than that, about something he has never understood.

This situation prompted me, once or twice, to make the effort to toss a small farthing among the offerings of others; but I noticed that the heap of them was so wide, and hollow, that it sank downwards so far as to remain unnoticed, and I determined that a neat, portable[1] "guide" of the type I am now devising would be much more useful.

It is true that there are many books already written on the subject of emigration; nevertheless, I do not know that any book has yet been written about this subject solely to meet the needs of the inhabitants of the Highlands,

"In the language to which we gave our love,
And whose replacement we shall not understand."

Moreover, I think that something of this sort would be exceedingly useful to the "emigrant," in many respects: — as a counsellor at the time of departure — as a guide along the way — as a tutor, and as a companion, in the new country. No doubt it is an important matter to undertake to tell the emigrant how to leave, how to arrive, and what to do after arriving; but I ought to be able to caution him about all of this,

"For I was over there, and I saw it."

I

MARKING

❧

────────────────────────────   ──────────────────────────────

Since I have now made known the responsibilities that I have
undertaken, I think that it is my duty, in the beginning section,
to mark out who is, and who is not, suitable for the journey and
for the country about which we speak, and that is Upper Canada;
for it is the area of the country which I am observing at present.
I am so eager to give good directions in this matter that I will
address the young women first.

For young girls, and for spinsters, I do not know, although it
is a great claim, if there is a land as good as America. Both work
and marriage are easy to be had for them there; and the work is
neither servile nor at all heavy. There is no mention of creel or
hoe, of the strand or peat bog in that place; and it is not fash-
ionable for women to be working outdoors there, at least no
farther than to bring a water pail or firewood through the door.
Poor service is the custom of the country, and four *dollars* a month
is the common wage a servant receives. I would advise every young
woman, who is neat, and who has permission to travel, to do her
utmost to get over there without delay. She need not take a bundle
of shoes with her, for footwear is as inexpensive over there as it

is here; but let her take plenty of clothes with her, if she is able, particularly of that sort that her mother and grandmother used to make, which some call *stuth*[2] while others say *camlet*.[3] This clothing is exceedingly useful in the winter, for it is warm and snug, and it is not prone to catch fire like cotton clothing. The spark which jumps from the fire (for there will be sparks as large as a pullet's egg exploding now and again from the fire in America) will go through a cotton gown as quickly as a musket ball would go through a winnowing-fan; but it will fall away from the *stuth* as if it met a coat of tempered mail.

Before I bid farewell to the young women, I say freely and clearly to the one who decides that she will not be obedient and useful to her mistress, or to her own husband (if one accidentally falls for her deceit), that she not go over there to deceive the unsuspecting; let her remain where they know her, and her ways. If she is not respected over here, she will not be any more valued over there, once they come to know her; and flitting from one residence to another every month is too troublesome and too costly in America.

People usually believe that the young man, who is not accustomed to manual labour at home, will not be of any use in America; but that is not the case. If he is solid, and sensible by nature – pleased to receive a small piece of land for himself, and has approximately one hundred pounds sterling to start, – he may get on well, particularly at clearing land. And why not? he is just as knowledgeable as, and much easier to instruct in that work than the man who has spent twenty years as a ploughman in Scotland. But if he hires servants with his money, with the intention of keeping his hands in his pockets while he oversees them, he will go bankrupt and will be a poor man in a moment. What he needs is to buy land, an axe, oxen, a hoe, a harrow, seed-corn, and food; to build a home and barn with the money; and to do the work with the sweat of his own brow, until he is capable of paying his servants' wages with the fruit of his labour. If he does not undertake to do all of this, he is not fit to go over; let him remain as he is.

Let the young man who is a good labourer be not at all anxious about going to America, even if he has not a single coin with him, except to pay the passage. He will get work as soon as he sets foot on the land, and a good wage too – from a half dollar to a dollar a day – from ten to thirty dollars a month – from twenty to forty pounds sterling a year. From this, it can be seen that the wages will permit the high price of clothes there, expensive as they are, just as they do here, or even a little more so. But a man need not bother, having newly arrived in the country, to expect a high wage; for he does not deserve it, until he learns the work of the place. It is a very sad matter for a man of the sort I have just mentioned to be living in poverty here as long as the like of America is available to him. Let him depart then; and if he is prudent, in a short time he will have something which no other man can take away from him, as long as Britain remains foster-mother to Canada.

The man who is unemployed and a poor labourer, who is of no use to himself or to any other man – who takes no pleasure in anything honourable, but goes about with a gun, poaching deer and doing other unlawful things of the same nature – let him stay where he is; I will not ask him to come to a country that is not suitable for him. However, if "that which put the roe into the loch" persuades him "it is time to be off,"[4] my advice for him is to avoid it: – Let him give a half crown to the smith to see if he can make a chain or pot-hook from his gun, from which he can hang the potato pot. He may take the shoulder belt with him just as it is, for if he ever gets oxen, it will be useful to him to tie a bell to one of their necks. A gun! that is something I would not expect any man to bring, except one man alone – that is one who has a great deal of money, and who does not know what to do with it. He may indeed bring a gun with him; for I have often seen that when money belongs to that type, the gun will likely be present.

Rich or poor, young or old, I do not welcome the man who is fond of strong drink. No; for I would not care to wish a short life on him. The country in which I purchased a bottle of brandy (though I did not drink it myself) for a shilling, and in which I often earned four shillings a day, would I ask this man to go there? No; but let him spend his time for three years in the Temperance League, then let him go back again, and his wife and children will bless him.

Every Shoemaker – Cooper – Smith – Cartwright – Joiner – Shipbuilder – Tailor and so forth, who is not faring well at home, would be wise to leave immediately; for tradespeople will do exceedingly well in America. Their daily wage was between a dollar and a dollar and a half whenever I travelled the country; that is, from four to six shillings in our money. There is no need at all for Shepherds, unless they begin farming; but if they do, and they are able men, they will do as well as any other sort. There are many Merchants and an over-abundance of Innkeepers prospering in Canada. Weavers are, in a sense, like the Shepherds; there is no great need for their services; but I knew a few Highlanders among them who began clearing land, and who were coming along exceedingly well. These were stout, robust men, well-trained from youth for earning a wage; but I would not think that the thin, delicate ones in the cities would be of much use there. As for Fiddlers, Pipers, and Musicians, and the like, America will not suit them; the common people are not so foolish as to throw their wealth away on whimsy without there being any benefit. There are no Beggars, and if the Tinkers have found their way over, I have not seen any of them, nor have I come across their work or their horn spoons.

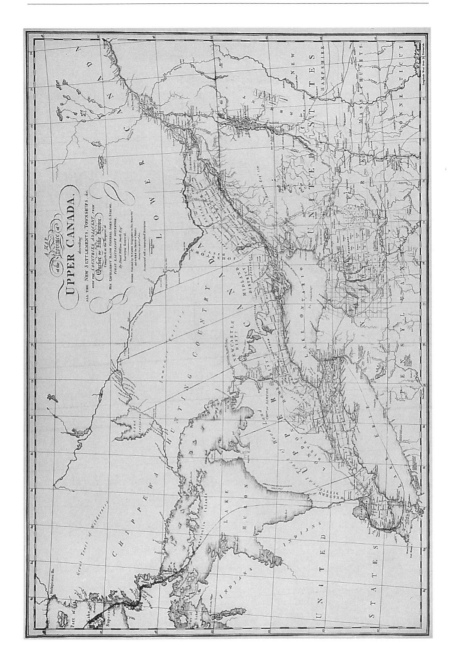

*A Map of Upper Canada, David William Smyth, Esq., Surveyor General General,
2nd. ed., 1813.* Courtesy of the Association of Canadian Map Libraries,
Facs No. 12. Public Archives of Canada.

As for every man past the age of military service (fifty-six), though he be as fit as an otter, I would not urge him to go overseas; unless he has one or two daughters who have not yet been given in marriage, and so forth. Either that, or he should have a brave crew of young lads, capable of turning their hands to working the land, sailing, or fishing. The age when they are most useful to the fathers who go to America is from ten to eighteen years. Certainly, the twelve-year-old, if he is raised as he ought to be (something, though shameful to say, that is happening much too rarely among the Gaels), is nearly as useful as a man at the peak of his strength. But in any case, if the man of whom we are speaking has a family like this, it is hard-hearted of him to keep them here, as most of them will fail because of his selfishness, and it is not only to them that he does a disservice; for the children would be much more able to assist him over there than they will be here.

But, alas! there is still another man whom I must advise. But what can I say to him, since I have already lost all expectation of his going over? He reminds me of a lean cow in the spring, who, having gone into a bog, makes one or two attempts to reach the solid, stony ground, but when she does not succeed as well as she had hoped, she lets out a heavy sigh; she casts a weary glance at the hillock before her, and, then, accepts her situation as best she can. This, and no other, is the man who is stuck on a tiny piece of land in the Highlands, paying, let us say, from two to fifty pounds sterling in rent, and even from eighty to one hundred in some places. This is just the man who needs America, and America is just the country that needs this man. It is, certainly, a truly grievous matter to see the overwhelming despair of many of these people throughout "the Glens" who have nothing, I may add, for their labours; they and their families cultivating a patch of poor land that will not support servants' wages; not only that, but land which would not pay servants' wages even if no rent at all were required; and, moreover, that would not support a family properly, even though the family owned the place from the ground up. Such people are worn out raising their children to begin with; moreover, their children are wasting their time here with them, and in the end will be worn out supporting them, with nothing in the world to show for all the painful and troubling effort they have made. Things will ultimately be so bad that they will not be able to leave the country, even though they be eager to do so; the son will toil more than the father but remain much poorer. How different is the family's situation in America! where the son need not become weary assisting the father, if that were the situation, but it is not; rather, it is the father who assists the son, for the son will inherit not only the father's land but the results of his labour as well. The man who raises a family in America has a sense of satisfaction that the Highland tenantry do not understand. Although he may start out at a disadvantage, he will continually improve his situation, and this will strengthen his courage to overcome every hardship he may encounter. Although he may come home weak and weary on a Saturday evening, when he returns to the situation on the following Monday, and he sees anew, as it were, what he accomplished the past week, he will say to himself that no other man will take this from him in his lifetime, nor from his descendants after his death; no man lacking experience in this matter will understand his thoughts. Many *long* days will come when the memory of working on other people's land will be foremost in his mind, as well as the sum he paid them per year in order to receive permission to work on it. This will lead him to remember the people he has left behind him doing the same work, and the wretched state of anxiety they are in, fearing that if they do not cultivate the *croft* well, they will not have enough to maintain winter provisions; fearing that if they do improve the croft, some other man will offer a crown extra for it, and their work will be lost: he will sigh at first, pitying their wretched state; then he will smile a little, mocking them for their foolishness, and he will start "giving thanks on the good day" for his own circumstances.

Now before I let this portion of the matter of emigration slip from my hands, I would like the Reader to understand fully that I am not in any way asking the man who is *very well off* here to leave; I would advise him to remain, even though he wished to leave. Neither will I encourage the man who would only leave against his will: he has some idol or other over here, and it would be well for him to stay near it. The man who is wealthy in land over here — yet is not happy, since he does not have a finger in the *sweetness* of the land over there as well — let him remember,

"Though the one-eyed dog be longing,
Will he not be served as well on this side as on that."

Let him learn to be thankful for what he has, and let him remain in a familiar place.

II

PREPARATIONS, &C.

I would think that by now I have a chance to raise my head after carefully marking with *keel* the shoulders of my entire flock of sheep.[5] If I have marked them with *keel*, this shows I have undertaken their delivery. If I have undertaken their *delivery*, then I must take charge of my flock as in the days of my youth, to the point of deciding their *fold* is no longer good enough for them. I will be looking about me for the best way, and the cheapest way, to get them to the pasture I have intended for them; but since sea and bog lie before us, it will be necessary for us to prepare for the journey beforehand.

Every man who is going on this journey, then, let him bring, if he can, the following things: - plenty of protective clothing and bed clothes — stockings — broad blue bonnets, the type which the northern Highlanders call *sgrath*[6], the Glengarry bonnet need not take the passage — a large bolt of cotton cloth for shirts - coarse woolen fabric for white vests — blanket fabric for knee breeches — thin canvas fabric for summer trousers. These would be worthwhile provisions, for these things are almost twice the price in Canada. Also, augers — gimlets — one or two spades of the strongest variety — a few iron nails to have on hand on the

way, and after arriving. As for the smaller carpentry tools, such
as a plane, chisels, and so on,[7] there is no need to bring them
with him. The emigrant will not get the time to trifle with carpentry in Canada. Even if he attempted it, he would break the
tools with the amount of difficulty he would have trying to use
them, and that would be a great loss after paying the price of
passage. A man would do better to get a craftsman to do work
of this nature, for then he would get it done right, without
losing time at it himself. This is ultimately the cheapest method
in America.

With regard to pots and cooking utensils, if the emigrant
himself is to be preparing his own food going overseas, it will be
necessary for him to bring some of these with him; if not, I would
not advise him to buy them over here: but if he happens to have
them already, it is just as well for him to keep them for his needs
in the new country. A roasting pan, the kind they have in the
Highlands, will not be of any earthly use over there. Tin plates
are too expensive there, and neither are the kind they make there
any good: I would consider it prudent for a man to bring them.
He should not take over an axe at all, for Scottish smiths do not
know how to make any that would be of any use.

The emigrant ought to place everything that he is bringing with
him neatly in square chests, not too large, or in barrels, and to
be exceedingly careful with his possessions when boarding a ship,
especially if he is sailing from a city; for the rabble usually gather
around that sort of situation, and every one of them is angling
for anything he can get his paws on to snatch away suddenly.

A variety of food is exceedingly pleasant, and also necessary
at sea; and every man who goes forth into the Atlantic Ocean
ought to make the utmost effort to bring a little of each type of
provision he can gather up. I am not at all recommending this to
emigrants to make gluttons of them. I am actually cautioning
them about variety because I know it is requisite for their health,

and because I am of the opinion that the harbour is a terribly
incommodious place for emigrants on their journey. Men ought
to be watchful of their provisions after going on board also; for
"the mischief is not all on Bute": there will be a deceitful sheep
in the flock, even after going to sea, nor is this at all surprising.

III

FARES, &C.

There is seldom a country, or a port town in a country, that does not have its own unique fares with regard to emigrants, according to its situation and its individual facilities. It is possible to understand the reason for this, and see that it is logical, by examining other types of markets. Which emigrant does not know that he can purchase a three-year-old ox on Lewis or on Uist for one pound sterling less than he will pay on Falkirk moor? Similarly, who, having the slightest inkling about the geography of these districts, would consider it surprising that emigrants are sent over from Leith and Aberdeen for one pound sterling less than from Greenock or from Glasgow? But since the west coast of Scotland is most convenient for the Gaels, I will show them a general system of *fares* in recent years in that region: —

	Pounds	Shillings	Pence
Adults	2	15	0
Those under fifteen years	1	7	6
Children under five years	0	13	9
Infants and young orphans	0	0	0

The skipper will have to pay four shillings a head, in addition to this amount, to the emigrants' infirmary when he reaches the other harbour. This is an excellent system; and it is necessary for many a poor Gael, even though some, without thinking, complain when parting with the money. If a sick man lands anywhere in America, he will be taken into these houses (for there are houses of this sort in every port town); and if any man has weak family members, and he is in great distress for lack of money, and he is not able to proceed to his intended destination, he will be relieved either with money, or with work being provided for him then and there.

IV

ADVICE CONCERNING THE EMIGRATION OF THE GAELS, &C.

❧

Telling a story is a thing which has an exceedingly curious effect on the mind, particularly if a person tells it whole-heartedly; for the man who relates it imagines that he can see everything happening exactly as it was, is, or will be. This is just how I am at this moment; for I imagine I see my countrymen setting their course from Barra Head, and heading out to the expanse of the ocean, in good spirits. If they were to do that, the day would be favourable for the wretched creatures. But although it would be a reason for thankfulness to them, and a matter of satisfaction to me, I would not want to see it happen, for all that, unless there were one or two gentlemen with them, who had a more honourable profession than "guide." Just as I would show little respect for the flock if I did not permit it shepherds, so too, I would show little concern for the interests of the Gaels, if I did not permit them watchmen, hard-working, evangelical ministers, to explain the word to them which is "able to make them wise for salvation," in their mother tongue, the only language understandable to the Gaels; and who would make themselves worthy of the Gaels' love with their degree of diligence and faithfulness in cautioning them about "the one thing which must not be forgotten"; and moreover, who would be "in meekness instructing those who would stand against them." And it would not only be ministers who would vouchsafe my hope for the Gaels. There is another special group of gentlemen that I would like to send along with them, that is the schoolmasters — gentlemen to whom the Gaels have never given the esteem or respect befitting them, and on whose work they have never bestowed the notice or time it has merited. For this error, the Gaels' excuse will not be accepted,

> For they "may see each day,
> That this raised up the English."

The school is the hearthstone of the house of knowledge and information; and if the hearth of the house does not get swept clean and is not kept in good order, what hope do we have at all of gathering at the threshold? It is the schoolmasters who gird us up and prepare us to make our way through life as is proper for heroic men, and for Christians. It is they who make the ministers' yoke, to a large extent, tolerable. And it is not only the ministers' yoke they are making more bearable, for they take on a measure of the parents' burden as well. Were it not for the schoolmasters, we would not know where America is, or even how to reach it; and to make a short story of it, were it not for them, we would be exceedingly ignorant of our duty to God and humanity; —

> "For, although those great and small among the people,
>   Had enough Bibles,
> If they did not know how to read properly,
>   They would gain no knowledge from them."

If Highland emigrants were so fortunate, then, or as I ought to say, so sensible, as to bring both the minister and the schoolmaster along with them, they would be doing themselves and their

descendants who would come after them a favour. I do not at all
mean that they can do this, nor that they should try, with the
method of travel available at this time. It would be impossible
for five families from this parish, for three from the other parish,
and so on, to bring a minister and a schoolmaster with them; but
if they departed as they ought – that is, every man who is able,
from the length and breadth of the parish (for any poor man,
who wants work, ought not to stay, if he can leave) – turning
out with one accord at the same freight vessels (and the passage
would be much cheaper then, as well) – gathering every provision they would need, such as *tea, sugar,* &c., duty-free – and above
all, settling themselves over there in the same place, side by side,
without accepting the mixing of black, white, or yellow (for they
are all there in Canada), inside their borders, at least no farther
than to give a night's lodging – they would be able to acquire
teachers; and, by making this arrangement, they would be able to
bring them as well. This is how Glengarry, in Upper Canada, was
settled when that famous gentleman, Bishop Macdonell, who
died last year in Dumfries, departed on behalf of the Gaels.
They are today in as good a state as they might have wished –
they have plenty to eat and drink of meal and milk, and of everything else that grows in that area. English writers do not give them
much praise as farmers. Nor can I praise them in that way; but
I will say this, that I would like any other man to tell me where
in America an emigrant will be accepted as hospitably, and as
cheerfully, as he will be in Glengarry, – and who gave more
support to Britain than the people of that place when the rebels
revolted against us in the year 1837. Although the Bishop was a
very old man at that time, he stood for them just as dutifully as
he had in the previous war. He was always prepared to advise them
in peace, and guide them in battle; and though it is often said
that he could help them only as "the kite watches over the hens,"
those well acquainted with the Bishop knew that he always had

the good of his countrymen in mind. We are not denying that
he was not "licking his fingers" with each great affair in which
he was involved; and why should he not? I wonder, if he were
not, would another man not be doing the same?

The Gaels in *Pictou*, New Scotland[8], also gathered together in
this manner, in the same area where,

> "MacGregor of the verses, victories, and blessings,
> Who was meek and mild in manner,"

lived. It was this James MacGregor who composed those pleasant verses we have in Gaelic, and who wrote many a sermon just
as good as the verses, in their own place, in their *Pictou* and its
environs. His effect was obvious; the Gaels were peaceful and safe
there, until nature took its course, and age mercilessly began to
render him unfit for the work. And, when he went the way of all
flesh, the Gaels dispersed throughout the entire country. Perhaps
some went to a better place; but they might not have done so
well there, after all that.

I saw, in one place after another in America, occasions where
men went over in groups like this, as we are advising the Gaels to
do, and I know of no place at all where they did not have sufficient dwellings in a short time, except for the large, improper emigration Lord Selkirk sent to the Red River; and with regard to
that, a different outcome should not have been expected, for, as
the wren said to the eagle, "when you hear a story without substance, don't believe it." I know of one particular place in Upper
Canada which was settled like this, that is *Waterloo*. The Dutch who
came to America from Holland about twenty-five years ago, live
in *Waterloo*. They did not know a word of English at that time,
and not many of them speak it yet; but that did not harm them,
for they had a minister with them who was quite fluent: and he
needed to be; he had their complete confidence. The minister gave

them guidance along the way — he translated for them in every bargain, until every one of them was on his site, and for many days and years after that. He chose and marked out the land he judged most suitable for them — he married their youth — he baptized their children — and he preached the gospel to them, and to every creature who came near him, through his speech, and in his manner of living. Today *Waterloo* is a region that could grace any small kingdom, with flour and meat as cheap as anyone could ask for, and the apples as plentiful as the potatoes.

Since I am now about to bid farewell to everyone and everything on this side of the Ocean, and to take one leap forward without reservation, in order to smooth out everything which might cause the emigrant to stumble when he arrives, I would pray of the Gaels, before we part, that they leave in groups, as I have directed them; for, in so doing, the youth will not be in danger of falling into bad company, which is much too commonly seen in America. Although it is an unpleasant, and lamentable matter, nevertheless, I would not be fulfilling my duty if I did not take this opportunity to caution the emigrant regarding his behaviour when he enters the new country; for America, more than anything else, is a country in which "the one thing that is needed" is terribly far from sight. In the everyday speech of some persons there are curses as repulsive as any ear has ever heard; and where these are heard, other consequences will follow: but the decent man will protect the man who seeks good companions, and who has understood that "godliness is valuable for all things," and that it is "necessary always to pray and not to faint." There are many good ministers and teachers over there also, here and there. They are from many countries, and of many languages; but much more abundant even than that are their religious persuasions — Highlanders, Lowlanders, English and Irish, Dutch, Germans, Americans, Africans and Indians, and many others which the narrow limits of my small book will not permit me to mention. It would not surprise me if the emigrant said at this point, "And why would we take teachers over, if they are already there?" But the emigrant should rest upon his ease; he may be over there till he goes gray without ever seeing one of them.

V

QUEBEC, &C.

❦

The emigrant who sets off from "the bay of barks" to go to America by way of *Quebec,* need not expect to see land at all when he first arrives in the country, or that there will be an anchorage near at hand when he gets into the mouth of the river (*St. Lawrence*), for it is not emptying out of a mere millrace. Certainly not; and it is necessary for merchants and emigrants alike, that Providence sees fit to have the river travel with a slow, measured pace when it comes to cast its *drops* into the sea; for if it received an order to put distance behind it with all its might, the steam of its breath would set almost a hundred miles of seal islands boiling when it arrived. And why would it not be able to do all this, and more if it had to, when it must travel almost a hundred miles from one side to another, before it can finally deign to say, "This is my journey's end?" This will give the emigrant a correct idea of the full extent of the country which can always keep this channel of water full, particularly when I tell him that, even though he spent a hundred days walking up its banks, at twenty miles a day (and that would not be exaggerating, as it is through forests, brooks, &c.), I do not know whether it might still not be easier for him to head for what he has left behind rather than for what lies ahead.

When the emigrant reaches the gulf of the *St. Lawrence*, he is leaving *Cape Breton* behind him to his left and *Newfoundland* to his right. *Quebec* is a voyage of six days, or perhaps a voyage of six weeks, without the advantage of fair winds overhead; and before he arrives, the Gael will see things very similar to, and also very dissimilar from, what he has left behind. He will see hills raising their heads, as if they were trying to rise higher than the trees in the deer forest. From far away these are very like the hills of Scotland. But when the emigrant approaches them, he will see that the trees and branches of the forest have gained victory over the hills, for the forest stretches above their summits, going as high as the highest projection of land. When he leaves *Anticosti* Island a day or two's journey behind him, a foreign *guide* will meet him; this man will guide him safely into *Quebec*. With that I will stop giving advice; so that I may set out for land, in order to procure quarters for him when he arrives.

The Lower City of Quebec, from the Parapet of the Upper City, Charles Hunt, from a drawing by Lieutenant Colonel Cockburn, 1833. Courtesy of the J. Ross Robertson Collection, Metropolitan Toronto Reference Library. T14896.

When emigrants reach the desired harbour, the heads of families and young men are usually quite ready to land, and also to
leave their belongings on board the vessel — a practice which is
not at all wise. Nevertheless, I know that the Gaels who are not
used to being at sea will be ready to fall into this error; and since
they will, I would say that when any person goes on land, he
should not go there like someone playing the fool, but as someone
going on business — every house which does not have a clean, handsome appearance on the outside, between walls, windows, and
doors, is to be avoided; and though a house appears somewhat
clean, if the man sees one or two drunk men stumbling about on
the threshold, and unsavoury persons standing inside the door-
ways, so that both sides of the entrance seem to be laughing at
him, he is best to ward off evil by avoiding that house. No person
should let on that he has just come across the ocean, or people
will deceive him. There is no need at all for a person to confess
the truth to a stranger in *Quebec*. A person should inquire, in a few
decent-looking houses, about where to find inexpensive lodging
for himself and his family for one or two nights; and when he
arranges this matter to his satisfaction, let him return to the ship.
He should take everything he has ashore, and should be extremely
careful, for there are people there whose occupation is to plunder
strangers. In this fashion, a cautious person may make good use
of the time in which many other men will lose all their earthly
possessions, as I have seen happen there before. Any person about
to go westward ought not to tarry long in *Quebec*; nevertheless, he
will be none the worse for spending a day or two getting his legs
after spending five, or perhaps even seven weeks, at sea. The food
is not expensive there, and there are many things worth going to
see around *Quebec*. The emigrant will see many unusual things there.
The houses are roofed with tin, instead of the slate they use here;
and although the first part of the town he sees is not overly pleas-

The Citadel of Quebec, W.H. Bartlett, in Willis' Canadian Scenery, *1848.*
Photography by Axel Menzefricke.

ant, when he ascends the hill, he will get a beautiful view of the river and of the surrounding country. He will see *St. Rooks* beside the bay to the north, and *New Liverpool* just opposite, on the other side of the river. When the sun shines on the buildings of these towns, the tin on their roofs will give off an exceedingly brilliant radiance, especially after midday, when the sun descends in the west. If he ascends to the Plains of Abraham, above the town, he will have a not bad view. Many travellers say this is the most beautiful place they have ever seen; and I do not expect that anyone who sees it will say such men have given it more praise than it merits in that regard. As for me, if I did not have the biography of the poet, I would believe he was on the Plains of Abraham when he sang —

> "Every street with the most resplendent greens,
> Like a king's *palace* surrounding them;"

and I still imagine he must have been dreaming of it, or of some-where else quite similar to it when he penned those words. The emigrant will see there where *Wolfe*, the famous and noble mili-tary commander, fell and was buried[9]; as well as many other places, in which great and wonderful things took place, in the clash of heroes that day. A good view of the Fort can be obtained there also — the strongest fortification I believe Britain has, exclud-ing *Gibralter*. But it was not made so strong by human ingenuity; rather, it was naturally suited to this use. I cannot say how high it is; but it seems quite likely to me that the summit of the hill on which it is built, is three times as high as the rock on which Edinburgh Castle is built. This hill is so close to the river that there is space for only one row of houses, and for a narrow roadway at its base, on the other side; and the face of the rock is so steep, that it cannot be climbed without a ladder. Therefore, it is easy to see that this fortification is not easily attained by land; and from the water it would be impossible, for I would think that even if there were only a team of young boys up above, with a pile of stones near at hand, they could push the strongest fleet that ever sailed, back out to the ocean depths. The river is not too wide here, nor does it run too rapidly. Steamships ferry across between *Quebec* and *New Liverpool*; but boats of every other type are more plentiful, engaged in every kind of occupation they can get around town; and there are hundreds of British vessels throughout the summer and fall, seeking timber, &c. Fish are quite plentiful along the whole river; and that is exceedingly convenient for the settlers of Lower Canada, for not many of them eat meat during a particular time in spring - that is, from the night of Shrove Tuesday until Easter Sunday. Therefore, fish are both plentiful and in great demand; but, on the other hand, that leaves meat cheaper to buy.

Edinburgh Castle, Engraved by J. Jackson, from an Original Drawing by J. Knox, in One Hundred and Fifty Woodcuts, *1835.* Photography by Axel Menzefricke.

VI

INDIANS, &C.

When a Highland herdsman, from the hills, leaves a place around May Day, and takes service with a new master, as soon as he arrives, and sees the appearance of the area, the first thing he wonders is, what does the herd look like — are these livestock better than the livestock he has left behind — what kind of grazing practices do they have here — will the cattle be in danger of breaking out of this field into that other one — and so forth. Is it not natural to think the emigrant will be of the same mind concerning his fellow creatures when he reaches the new country, where he will see a type of people who are, without a doubt, of a different *race* from that which he left behind in the land of the thistle; for he will see all of this realized in the Indians.

But although the Indians are a different colour than the Gael, they are neither *black* nor yellow, as some maintain. Neither are they the colour of copper, nor can I name anything that I have ever seen that is exactly their colour; but I hope, nonetheless, that I can tell how to make something that is their colour. When one of my kinswomen in the Highlands is dyeing cloth, let her take hold of a hank of yarn; let her immerse it in the tub of lichen; let her wring it tightly, and firmly, when she lifts it out; then let her immerse it twice more in the pot of dyer's woad, wringing it carefully each time she lifts it out; and I would almost bet my share of the cloth that there is not an artist in the city of the King of *France* who could produce anything closer to the hue of their complexion.

But even if a Gael were loath to compare the Indian's appearance to his own appearance, it would not be offensive for him to do so; for it is perhaps regarding the Indian that they said, this was truly a

Man "bodily of the most resplendent figure,
Without any defect in form."

The Indian's hair is blacker (if that is possible) than "the raven of the mountain dell," each strand as rough as a piece of the shaggy hair of the gray horse – his alluring blue-black eyes could grace the face of princes, just like the earth berry, with regard to colour. His shoulders are broad, his chest deep, his body neat, and his form is without fault above the knees; but every single one of them has an outward bend in the calves; and the reader will understand the cause for this before we part company. The men among them walk elegantly and cheerfully, with backs as straight as a rod of ewe wood; but the women have a heavy, undulating gait, like the Highland women who are used to carrying the creel. It is their burden that fosters this gait in the Indian women also, for the men do not carry so much as a whirligig of the family provisions. When they wish to move camp (something that is not at all difficult to do), every man takes his gun and hound, his shot and powder, his bow and quiver of arrows; and he will have nothing to do with anyone or anything else, save those alone. This freedom belongs to the young man of twelve years of age as well as to the father, if that young man has demonstrated his prowess in hunting deer, beasts, or fishing; but the women and girls have the business of carrying the small children, and of keeping up with them on the way, along with carrying every other worldly possession in the dwelling, from the dwelling covers, to pots, clothes, food, and skins. When they reach their destination, or when night forces them to take rest, they grab hold of the *tomahawk*[10] (tuagh-bheag)[11], cut down approximately two dozen poles, tie all of the tapered ends together correctly also, and then raise them as straight as possible. When they get them standing on their base like this, one man scrapes a circular furrow around them, as with a compass. Then every man and woman present takes hold of the base of a pole, and everyone lifts out the base of his own pole until it reaches the furrow. Then they drive the bases of the poles into the furrow, and take hold of the coverings. The coverings are not difficult at all for them to handle; for they can often be like large bolts of cloth, perhaps thirty yards long, woven with dried grass, bark, &c., something like straw cloth. This is their way of putting the covering on - one man takes one end, and he puts a pin in it, and fastens it around a pole; another man wraps the other end of it four times around the poles, continually taking it higher; the rest sew the bottom edge of the upper circuit to the top edge of the lower circuit with pins, and so on in this fashion, until they reach the top. When they reach the top, they leave a small hole, without a covering, for a smoke hole, and they leave another gap open between two of the poles for a door, and in that way their tent is fully set up in less than half an hour.

The Indians are not overly attentive to what they put on their heads or on their bodies, but they like to pay very good attention to their feet. They usually wear a cap, and an overcoat, of coarse, white, English flannel in winter in *Canada,* a red belt tied about their waist, and scarlet red hose, like those that young ladies wear in Scotland, with both ends open between the calf and the base of the thigh, and nice sandals on their feet, made

Indian Lodges on the Beach of the Island of Mackinac (Lake Huron, U.S.), 1837, Anna Jameson. Courtesy of the J. Ross Robertson Collection, Metropolitan Toronto Reference Library. T14975.

of, and sewn with, deer skin. They call these *mocassin* (mu chasen)[12], and I really do not think that a person can put any other footwear *mu chasan* that is half as warm and comfortable as they are: to make the story short, the emigrant will not do well without them in winter in America.

The Indians are a nation skillful in deer hunting and fishing, and that is really no surprise, since most of them do nothing else from birth to death. They recognize the part of the forest which the deer frequent, and when they happen on such a place, they find a hollow-tree[13], digging out a hole in it which a good marksman can get into; at that time, the others cover the hole, except for the area in front of his eyes, with bark so similar to the rest of the tree, that a deer or pole-cat will never recognize that a *tomahawk* was used on it. When everything is right, the others depart and leave him in the tree, and when the deer come, he will have a stag with the first shot. This method would be as good on a bare hilltop; but the deer do not come out in the open in the forests of *America*.

They fish mostly in the winter, and this is usually how they go about it. One man takes a *tomahawk* and cuts a round hole in the ice, approximately twenty inches in width; at the surface he sets up a rod or two which he has bent and tied somewhat like the framework of a pannier basket; he sets a cluster of lopped-off tree branches on the ice at the edge of the hole, and a few hides on top of that. He lies down at the hole with the hides under him; he fastens one corner of the top hide across the rods, and then, when he looks in under it, he will see thirty fathoms down in the water, as clear as the light of noonday. But as good as his eyesight may be, that will not lure the fish to him, and he must use another device, and he has just the device to use. A small model of a herring, made of wood, with scales, fins, and gills; a bit of lead is set inside it, keeping it level, and a fishing line is tied to its back, keeping it upright. He holds the fishing line himself in his left hand, and with every move he makes, the model will move with his movements, and any man alive, who did not see it go down as a piece of wood, would think that it had life in it, as surely as the fish in the ocean are alive. When the large fish comes around and sees the Indian's wooden herring, it will think, as we ourselves often do, "that the one with the quickest hand gets the best portion," and it will rush at the herring; but if it does, the misfortune it meets will be all its own fault. The Indian will be waiting with a trembling impatience,

And "a straight, sharp fishing spear,
With its own attached *bow*,
    — In his fists."

It is possible for him to catch forty in half an hour, and it is also possible for him to be stretched out for the whole stormy winter's day without catching so much as a cuddy.[14] But there is one thing I know for certain; there is no other man who could stay so long waiting for a fish, or catch it so expertly when it comes.

But in spite of the many ways in which the Indians are skill-ful, their dignity is greatest raising their children. As soon as an infant is a day or two old, they wrap it comfortably in a piece of flannel cloth, they pull a small fold between its feet so that its thighs and calves (it is this which renders them bandy-legged) will not be too hot, they put a wooden collar around its neck, and another around its bottom, bound to the plank, and then they put a good, strong, tough leather strap through a hole at the top of the plank and hang it tidily on a hook on a pole. This is an exceedingly easy way to care for children, instead of rocking them in a cradle, teaching them to cry all day and night, unless someone makes it his occupation to dandle them. The Indians do not give them bad habits from the start, and since they do not, the children will not miss them. No sound is heard out of them from morning until night. There they are, neat and tidy, without so much as an earlobe to be seen,

But a pretty, crooked little nose,
And bare little toes,

out of the clothes. They have an excellent opportunity, up high like this, to look at everything going on throughout the house, keeping away their sorrows, and if they are hung on a tree outside, they will not want for company, even though they have only the wren and the robin red-breast. Although the Gaels do not use this method today, or a method as good as it, for rearing chil-dren, I do not know whether they have not used it in the past; if they have not, why would it be said: —

"She tied the infant to a board,
On top of a withered branch close to her"[15]?

They call an infant a *Papoos* (patha-bus)[16], and it is certainly a suitable name, for I do not think it is natural for any other *bus* to be always as *patha* as an infant's *bus*.

Although the Indian can stand his ground on the battlefield, he is not as good a soldier in the face of fire as he is in the hunt, taking up pursuit. This became known, in a notable way, the day of the battle at *Queenston* in *Upper Canada*. They were aiding the British that day, and as soon as they put the *Yankees* to flight, they pursued them so relentlessly, that they forced every foreigner before them over the edge of a great rock cliff in that area. That would suffice for us, but when a few of them looked down and saw some of the *Yankees* grasping hold of small bushes, growing here and there over the face of the rock, they raised the battle cry and jumped down; every man carried off a *Yankee* in passing, as a hawk would drop on a moor cock from a peak on the side of a glen, without any consideration at all that his own death were as certain as the death of the *Yankee* at the base of the rock: Thus, the enemy who turns his back on them, need not expect that sea or moor will save him.

The Indians have neither king nor governor, but a chief, just like the clan chiefs who were once among the Gaels. They are as quiet as little mice in the presence of this chief, and it would be a pity if they were not, for he is just as attentive to his kindred as a father would be to his only child. They often show this care, even to the point of death, as happened with a few of them who were in a band of kinsmen assisting the British, if my memory serves me correctly, at BROCKVILLE. *Tecumseh* (deadh-chuimse)[17] saw that the *Yankees* seemed likely to win, and he therefore spoke to the leader of the British army. "I see," he said, "that if we do not take precautions, they will get what their hearts desire, that wing over there will make the devastation complete if it is not stopped; but let me draw back a little with three hundred of my men, and I will go quickly, without protection, through the forest; I will

not be long on the way, and I guarantee that when I arrive, the
backs of the English will find that the itch has been removed."
"I do not understand how you can accomplish all that you expect,"
said the Englishman. "Never you mind; entrust the matter to me,
and you will see what will happen." "Yes, but I am not the man
to do that," said the Englishman. "If not, then stick with your
own calamitous strategy, and everyone will see how the day ends,
but I will not see it! I have a few hours left, and I decide not to
waste them! neither you nor any other man will see the defeat of
Tecumseh!" Having said this, he left; the fury of his breast blazed,
he raised a triumphant cry with a fierce shrieking that would put
fear and trembling into "fifty soldiers," and like a fiery bolt of
lightning, he burst into the midst of his enemies, taking *deadh-
chuimse*, with a gun at either side of him; for he was

"Striking them dead and maiming them,
And leaving them there, without breath,"

until he laid waste to the section of the battlefield he was on.
But, alas! "it takes many hands to do the work," although no other
man could do injury *to*, and although no other man could escape
from, *dheadh-chuimse* himself, in single combat; nevertheless, because
of their superior numbers around him in this uneven battle, his
enemies got the opportunity to wound him from behind; he was
losing blood quickly and growing increasingly weaker, so much
so that he had to move to the rear and descend the brow of a
hill, amid the mangled corpses sleeping in the field. It was not
long before his presence was missed by his kinsmen; one or two
men returned swiftly to see how he was. When they approached
him, each man leaned his weight on his spear, staring at him with
tears like drops of spring dew rolling down the side of his cheeks.
They noticed that he desired to say something. A man jumped
up hastily and lifted his head gently from the ground. "We are

Tecumtha (c. 1808), Benson John Lossing. Courtesy of the John Ross Robertson
Collection, Metropolitan Toronto Reference Library. T16600.

parting, my men," he said, "choose a chief!" "We are parting,
alas!" they said, "but we do not have to choose a Chief, as you
have but one son, and he your only child." "You have always been
a faithful people to me, and do not treat my final request with
contempt, I beseech you!" he said, "I pray of you! have nothing

to do with him, but choose another!" "We will not despise your request, we will certainly honour it! but will you not let us know why we should not accept your son?" "He is so like a *Saganash*[18] in form, that I fear he will be just like them in his mind, and that he will not be worthy of the people's trust!" As the words faltered in his mouth, the sleep of death hovered over his eyes, the British rushed to retreat, every man fled, and *Tecumseh* remained on the battlefield; but, as he himself foretold, he did not see it.

With that the emigrant can see the type of people the Indians are, commanding valiant men, but I do not ever expect to see men who are more respectful toward others. They have a slow, soft, pleasant speech, merely a branch of the Gaelic language, and if those who first wrote it down had been well acquainted with Gaelic, the two languages would look remarkably similar. But if one or two travelling preachers were sent out from England, through the mountains to learn Gaelic, and if after they had scarcely begun to acquire it, they gave themselves permission to write it down, and put it in print, it would be just as difficult to

Church at Point-Levi, W.H. Bartlett, in Willis' Canadian Scenery, *1848.*
Photography by Axel Menzefricke.

understand as the Indian language, and much more difficult for me to read.

But although their language has been spoiled by the foreigners, their intelligence has not been destroyed by them, for these foreigners served as a means of bringing many of them from darkness into light, inasmuch as they cast off the old man, along with his works, in two senses, I hope. They have done this outwardly, at any rate, for many of them have now abandoned the hunting, and every old custom that was unprofitable, and have begun building permanent homes in the same place. They do not cultivate large areas within a few years, as many other people do in America, but they have enough crops to provide food for themselves and their families. The minister and the schoolmaster are always situated in their midst, so that they are close at hand to each and every family. Many of them have a godly look, and I would like to believe that their situation is not without hope, even though they were recently strangers to the commonwealth of Israel, and strangers to the covenants of promise, without hope, and without a God in the world.

VII

MONTREAL, &C.

❧

Montreal is approximately one hundred and fifty miles beyond Quebec, but it does not take long to reach it, for all that, for there are steamships available every day, so that the emigrant need not stay long in port once he is ready for his journey. These steamships do not usually take more than twenty-four hours going up, and a dollar and a half is the fare they most commonly charge. They often stop to take on fuel at a village called THREE RIVERS, on the right-hand side of the river, and at another town, called SOREL, a short distance beyond that, on the left-hand side as a person goes up. Everything the emigrant will see on this journey is excessively similar, every farm, house and yard, house of worship and cemetery, being laid out in the same manner. They have raised terribly high steeples on the churches, and these, like their other buildings, are roofed with tin, so that the emigrant will think the stars have risen around him, when the sun shines on them, around three o'clock in the afternoon, on account of their height and the height of the river banks on which they are built. When a person has reached *Lake St. Pierre,* he will encounter a great many islands until he arrives in MONTREAL, and after leaving it as well. MONTREAL is built on an island in a very sheltered, warm area; for there is a round mountain[19] to the rear, protecting it from the north wind and turning the heat of the sun back onto it. This island and others nearby are formed by the river, which divides into *tri*[20] branches where the other river, called the OTTOWA (ath-a-tuath)[21] meets it a short distance beyond the town; but one can discern all of this from the name, MON-TRE-AL (Monadh thri allt)[22] Montreal, then, is a most handsome town, brimming over with food and drink, and with many types of work which are always easy for emigrants to find. I know Gaels who have gone there with nothing in the world but a shilling, who are wealthy men today, accustomed to the common language of that country, and independent of the world; but my advice to anyone deciding to go up country is simply to stay here as briefly as possible. There is a company in this town that sends emigrants up to KINGSTON for a single fee, and I believe that is the best way for a person to go. But there are two ways to get there, to wit, emigrants usually go up the OTTOWA by steamships until they reach a *black* river, which comes into it up

Junction of the Ottawa and St. Lawrence (near Cedars), W.H. Bartlett, in Willis' Canadian Scenery, 1848. Photography by Axel Menzefricke.

Steamer "Iroquois," 1831 (St. Lawrence River, Ontario), Charles Henry Jeremy Snider. Courtesy of the J. Ross Robertson Collection, Metropolitan Toronto Reference Library. T16106.

at GLOCESTER, called the RIDEAU (ruith-dubh)[23]. A canal extends the length of this river until it strikes LAKE ONTARIO at KINGSTON. But they do not use steamships on it; it is so narrow that only hauling skiffs[24] can do the job. There are two hundred and fifty miles between MONTREAL and KINGSTON by this route, one hundred and thirty-three of those being entirely in the canal, and I think that the standard fare is between twelve and fifteen shillings. By going up this way, the emigrant will be able to take his effects with him without much expense, but if he goes up by way of the St. Lawrence, he will encounter something different, for the river flows so swiftly in many places that no boat of any kind can go against it; so much so that they transport emigrants around some of it by carriages, on land, and the roads are so bad, that it is often disagreeable for a single man to go through in a carriage, not to mention the head of a family with all his personal effects. But the distance this way is only one hundred and eighty miles, and it is

Brockville—St. Lawrence, W.H. Bartlett, in Willis' Canadian Scenery, *1848.*
Photography by Axel Menzefricke.

the shortest and least expensive way for the man whose only concern is himself. Any man who goes up this way will get a good view of the Gaelic district, Glengarry. This is the first part of UPPER CANADA that he will encounter. The boats often take on fuel at LANCASTER and CORNWALL, two nice villages in the Glen. If a stranger enters one of those towns, all he needs to do to find any of Clan Donald is to recite his lineage down, or up, as I ought to put it, to his father, his grandfather, and the men who came before him; who can say now that there are no Gaels in America? There are many islands on the river up the entire route, until the arrival at JOHNSTOWN. Some of these are very lovely to look at, but most of them have only poor land. PRESCOT and BROCKVILLE are farther up from here, and when a person leaves BROCKVILLE a short distance behind, he will reach the lower end of LAKE ONTARIO. But with the great number of islands, a person scarcely knows this is a lake, until he leaves Kingston far, far behind him.

Scene Among the Thousand Isles, W.H. Bartlett, in Willis' Canadian Scenery,
1848. Photography by Axel Menzefricke.

But to return to the OTTOWA, as he nears its confluence, any
man who goes up that river, is going west-northwest, until he
reaches the head of the canal. He will see many beautiful places
here, such as POINTE FORTUNE, &c. He will find Chatham, a district in which there are many Gaels, as he passes it by on his left-
hand side.[25] But although I have friends here, I would never advise
you to stay here, or anywhere else on the OTTOWA; there is most
often only poor land there, and it is excessively cold in the winter,
beyond what a person who has never been there, or anywhere else
like it, could comprehend. When a man reaches the mouth of
the RIDEAU, he goes south-southwest and leaves STORMONT, GLEN-
GARRY, and LOCHIEL far behind him on his left-hand side. After
going through GREENVILLE[26] &c., the canal ultimately leads a
person straight into the town of KINGSTON.

VIII

KINGSTON, &C.

Kingston has one particular attribute that I have not seen in many towns in Canada, excepting there alone — that is how abundant stone is there; but stone in KINGSTON is as plentiful as slate is in Ballachulish; and it is the best stone for buildings as well. The result is that there are nice, large buildings, and neat, clean streets, and on the whole, it is a very decent little town. The land surrounding it is somewhat light, as is natural for stony land everywhere; but nevertheless, it has a very good reputation for crops, particularly for wheat. A great deal of sailing activity takes place around this town, while the lake is open, and since the canal has been built, there has been an increasingly large flow through it, of the regular traffic of people, goods, and everything else. All goods going up country are shipped out in boats; all grain, food, and people coming from farther upcountry are brought here by boat; moreover, there is a large fishery here, and it is very conveniently situated near *New York State*, for *Oswego* is directly opposite it on the other side of the lake. I cannot say how broad the lake is in this place, but I would think that it is not greater than seventy-five or eighty miles.

Kingston (Lake Ontario), W.H. Bartlett, in Willis' Canadian Scenery, 1848.
Photography by Axel Menzefricke.

The district called *Frontenac* is out behind *Kingston; Hastings* borders on it, and *Northumberland* is farther away again at the upper end of the *Trent* river. The emigrant will not see this river at all as he goes past, for it empties into the Bay of *Quinte,* a branch of the lake which he will leave behind him on his right-hand side. *Port Hope* is the first port town worth mentioning that is seen after leaving *Kingston.* It is a very lovely little town in the summer. It is situated on a high, dry foundation, and there is good land around it. There is regular sailing to and from it; and herring, salmon, and all varieties of lake fish are quite plentiful in the surrounding area. *Port Hope* is one hundred and ten miles from *Kingston* and sixty miles, I would think, from *Toronto.*

IX

TORONTO, &C.

❧

When the British began to shape every place as they saw fit in Canada, they began to give these places the names they saw fit as well. They leapt on *Toronto* and called it *York*; but as the proverb says, where there are two Malcolms, one of them is a fool. This was the case here, as every paper and letter written to *New York* in the States, would be misdirected to *York*; nor was that strange, for *York*, which was not two years old, was *newer* than *New York*, which was three hundred. When they saw that matters were not entirely satisfactory, they leapt again, scratched out *York* and called it *Little York*. They waited a while, but *Little* did the job very little better, and they had to return to the old Indian name, *Toronto*. Although it is a great claim to make, *Toronto*, as it is today, after all the difficulty it has come through, is the most elegant *tòr*[27] that Britain has in *America*. This town is built on a clear, dry foundation, something that a person should always consider when establishing a town in *Canada*; for if a man puts buildings on low, wet land, those who live in them will certainly be unhealthy and diseased, and neither will they be long in dying of their illnesses. But this is not the only good attribute of *Toronto*; I do not know of any good point that any other town in the country has that it does

Toronto, W.H. Bartlett, in Willis' Canadian Scenery, *1848.* Photography by
Axel Menzefricke.

not have. There is better land there than in the lower part of the
country, and it is not so cold; goods are cheaper there than in
the upper part of the country, and it is not so cold.[28] To make
a long story short, I do not know if I have seen another place in
British America in which I would rather live. And it is not just
the town which is excellent, for the country around it is very lovely
also. *Scarborough* is on one side of it, and *Trafalgar* is on the other
side. *Albion, Caledon, Erin, Esquesing,* and many other places, that are
quite good for crops, lie out behind it. Emigrants will find more
than enough uncultivated land to purchase by going a short distance back, and there is very good land there, but it is a great distance from the harbour. *Toronto* was the capital of Upper Canada
until the two lands were united, but now Canadians do not pay
it any more heed than any other town; nor will we, let us leave
it.

X

HAMILTON, &C.

❧

Hamilton is a small town, very lovely to see, and very healthful for agriculture. Built on a beautiful, level mountain plain of dry, sandy land, varying between the colours of rusty red and white, it is at the uppermost end of *Lake Ontario*. It is forty-two miles, over the best arable land, from *Toronto*, and one hundred and sixty from *Goderich* in the *Huron Tract* — that is, by taking the highway through the country, but by following the water around, I think it is as much as five hundred miles away. Any man about to go up that way by water, or by way of *Lake Erie*, ought not to proceed to *Hamilton* at all, but cut across from *Toronto* to the base of Abhainn-na-Gàirich (*Niagara*)[29], and there is a canal (*Welland*) from there by which he can get to *Lake Erie*. In this fashion, he can sail around the most southwestern end of Canada, and head towards the north again, until he reaches *Goderich* on *Lake Huron*. At any time, he can get up to *Sandwich*, at the base of *Lake St. Clair*, by way of a ferry boat; and the *Cuideachd Chanada*[30] has a boat that comes there once a week to seek out all provisions that the town needs, and emigrants, if it finds any. Around the upper end of *Lake Erie*, and from there to the lower end of *Lake St. Clair*, is the warmest spot in all of British America; although any healthy Gael will survive the cold of winter there well enough, it has its own faults, for all that. Most often there is only low, boggy land, which is subject to diseases and to summer frost; but, however, for the man who thinks it will suit him, and who intends to go there, I will *guide* him by way of another path; that is, let him go ashore at *New York*, and he will go up on a steamship from there as far as *Albany*, a distance of approximately one hundred and fifty miles. He will go from there as far as *Shenectady*, sixteen miles on a railway, and from there he will get on the *Erie canal*, without missing a beat, until he is at *Buffaloe*, on the lower end of *Lake Erie*. This entire journey will take only about eight days, and about eleven dollars in fare, the fee it cost me a few years ago, at any rate.

But to return to my story. *Hamilton* is a town that has many unique advantages; it is conveniently situated at the lake, and it is close to the country; a road has been cut away from it toward the south, past *Ancaster*, through *Oxford*, an exceedingly beautiful district, all the way over to London; and there is another road going west from it through *Beverly*, *Flamboro*, and *Waterloo*, all the way over to *Goderich*. Thus, the emigrant can see that there are several channels bringing water to *Hamilton*'s mill.

Guelph (Ontario), May 12, 1842, Unknown. Courtesy of the J. Ross Robertson Collection, Metropolitan Toronto Reference Library. T16942.

XI

GODERICH, &C.

When the emigrant leaves *Waterloo*, he will be in *Wilmot*; then he will come upon *Easthope*, and when he does, let him know that he is on the borders of the Canada Company. *Ellice* is the next place he will see, and he will recognize it when he sees it, without inquiring of his companion, for there is something there which will speak a warning to each Gael who takes this road, and which will keep him talking for many a day and year; it is my duty to explain this to the emigrant, and since it is, I will do so. When the Company began selling their own land in the *Huron Tract*, they filled, not only America, but nearly the whole world, with papers concerning it. It would take someone a little more knowledge-able than the ordinary man not to think that this place was a little bit of unspoiled nature at the "threshold of the universe." The winter was warm; the summer was hot; a mill was built, land cleared, roads made, and the first harvest would be enough to pay the farmer's labour for clearing the land; he would forevermore be a gentleman, even if he lived to be as old as Methuselah; and although the world were to be turned upside down, he would remain a happy man. But for him to acquire these great blessings, he would have to be an easily persuaded man, doubting nothing

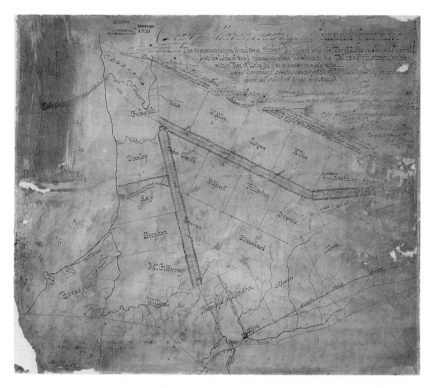

Draft of the Huron Tract Belonging to the Canada Company Showing the Communication Road from Goderich to the Talbot Settlement, John MacDonald, 1829 [map]; R61, B38 (SR 4750); Archives of Ontario; AO 1565. Courtesy of the Archives of Ontario.

of what he was told; he would have to believe that the raven were white on the eve of Shrovetide, that the black horse would eat its trough, and that providence would throw his way everything about which the hungry heart might secretly dream. He would be given land beside a road, and everything would be wonderful. It is about the time when this call rang deafeningly in the ears of European emigrants, that some of my countrymen who were about to emigrate overseas thought they might go to this place "beyond compare." They went, therefore, to the businessmen of the Company to see if there were *still* any piece they could get.

Yes, as *fortune* would have it, there was *still* a little left. One *map* was put up on top of another *map*, one on a table and one on a wall; there was a picture of every place over there, and, as it turned out, there was a picture of the spot about which we are speaking. This was truly a place abounding in resources. Every man, regardless of location, would prosper. What would it cost? the man who would not lift a hand to his wallet, lifted a hand for the *bill*[31], and every man left happily, with the number of his lot on a scrap of paper in his pocket. They set off, they and their families, despising what they left behind with "the old men wearing breeks," and decided they would neither stop nor rest until they could safely say,

"We will up and march away,
Whether others like it or not."

But when my young heroes reached their destination, what did they see? land that was not suitable for a living soul! if it were not for,

"A swarm of geese or ducks,
Draggling themselves in the mud with pleasure."

They began to clear a little land, and that was no small task. Anyhow, they managed to do it; they planted it, and harrowed it as well, but did they harvest it? no, it is not that the rain entirely drowned it in the spring, but the part that the rain did not finish off in the spring, the frost killed in the summer. After their labour, and the time lost on it over many a year, the poor, unfortunate people had to buy new land again from the Company, and leave the meadow as a wasteland, to serve as a lesson and warning to each emigrant who comes that way.

I have no doubt that the Reader is now just about as tired of the meadow as the people were who farmed it. And since he is, we will take a step along the path, and from now on, it will be a straight path. There are more than twenty miles here of road as straight as a map could draw it: that might well show a person how level the country is in this area. When a person proceeds approximately twenty miles, he will be in the district they call *Tuckersmith*, where there are many cheerful, hospitable Gaels. Most of these Gaels came up from *Pictou* in *Nova Scotia*, a place we mentioned close to the beginning of the book. Like all worthy Gaels, I have never seen them deny hospitality and generosity; but on the other hand, if a person turns on them, they are equally fierce in return: the "Guide" knows them every bit as well as the innkeeper knows the bottle. A walk of four hours will bring a person from the edge of *Tuckersmith* to the city of *Goderich*, the principal town of the *Huron Tract*.

Goderich is built on an excellent, lovely plain, of dry land of sand and gravel, on the banks of *Lake Huron*, a site as pleasant for a town, with regard to situation, as there could be in summer, but it is too exposed in the winter, especially as a foundation for a town in a country as cold as Canada. But what place does not have something to be avoided, and even if this place does, it has another good thing of which many of its neighbours cannot boast, which is the improvement of its harbour. This was a naturally sheltered harbour, and a great deal of money was laid out to develop it, so that it is now a "tranquil haven." But the worst thing about this area, even though the harbour is so good, is that there is not very much use for it yet; nor is it to be expected, for *Goderich* is only in its infancy; if my memory serves me correctly, they began building the first houses there in 1829, so boats have no business coming there for anything, since it does not yet have much to offer; and if they arrive there with a load, *Goderich* still has nothing to offer them in return. But although that is how things have been until now, there is every indication that *Goderich*

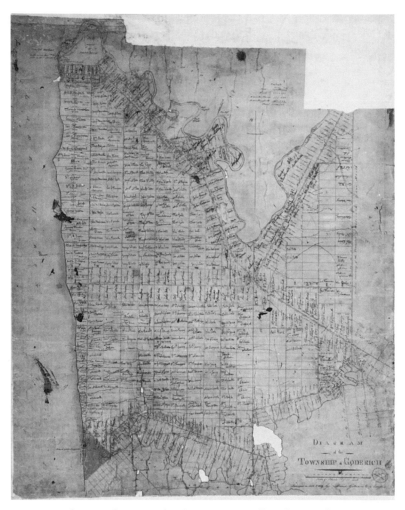

Diagram of the Township of Goderich, 1828, 1829 [map]; Canada Company Maps; OS 17, F129; Archives of Ontario; AO 4192. Courtesy of the Archives of Ontario.

will become a good town in time. The Company is making every effort that they can, in every way. They are cutting out roads, constructing bridges, building mills, and everything else they can, which they think will improve the area. As well as the road up which I guided the emigrant, they have constructed another to London, a distance of approximately sixty miles, and which was

Goderich, Ontario, 1858 by W.N. Cresswell. C-005132 National Archives of
Canada. AMS Imaging / National Archives of Canada. C5B2.

very difficult to level, for most of the land through which it goes
is too low-lying and soft. On the other hand, they are giving work
to poor men who do not have the means to pay for land with
money, but who will pay off every last farthing of it through
labour. They are taking a dollar and a half an acre for bush land
in new places, but where highways and other facilities of that type
are built, land will be much more costly. The price will always
be according to the improvement and the particular attributes of
each individual site, when a great deal of land in the area has
been cleared for sale. When they began selling the *Goderich* land
in the year 1830, it was a dollar and a quarter; but when the
"Guide" was last there, in the year 1839, it was four dollars an
acre, and I am quite certain that it is five today. Land is exceedingly good in this area, and there is often a heavy harvest if the
season is favourable, — particularly potatoes and oats; peas and
fairly good wheat grow there also, but wheat is a very uncertain
crop. A person may have a yield of thirty pecks to one peck of

seed, but perhaps more likely ten; nevertheless, it often far exceeds any other, for I know instances when there were thirty-four and thirty-five, several years. A respectable man, who was a good farmer, told me that he had forty, from time to time; and I believed him entirely. But potatoes now grow much better there than wheat, as far as I know. If they are planted in season, in freshly cleared land, forty barrels to a barrel of seed is not at all excessive, without fertilizing, weeding, or tilling, from the day they go into the ground till the day they come out. Barley does not respond well, but very productive rye does grow there, and everywhere else in Canada, I expect. Wonderfully strong and heavy oats grow there, as well, but they produce only a poor type of seed, nor are they trying to improve it; since none but horses, oxen, and pigs eat it in that district, it is not worth their while to bother much with it. Some plant Indian corn, but it is a very uncertain crop in that area; if the year is suitable for it, it may be worth the while, but if it is not suitable, it is a large undertaking for the man doing it to keep the corn alive for long. The area is not liable to summer frost, nor is it unhealthy, and it has another advantage which would be enough to beautify any place in America. There is water as good as anyone could ask for; I know of many a spring which would be enough to set a small mill in motion, coming up like a whirlpool through the gravel, as on the shoulders of Ben Doran. The forest is rough and tall, with many species of wood, but the sugar [tree][32], in particular, is especially plentiful.

But in spite of every good natural feature *Goderich* has, and in spite of what the Company has done for it, it also owes a debt to many of the men who went there while it was developing into a town. Many of these were rich men, exceedingly eager to promote the good of the area, and they spent their money clearing land, raising buildings, and on other works of that nature, which were

Yours truly, W. Dunlop (1833), Daniel Maclisse, 1898. Courtesy of the J. Ross Robertson Collection, Metropolitan Toronto Reference Library. T16707.

much more profitable to the area than they were to themselves. Among these were two kind gentlemen, *Captain* and *Doctor Dunlop*, two brothers, who bought and cleared land on the other side of the river which runs into the harbour, at the north end of town₃₃. One of these men was chosen by the people of the Huron Tract, in 1835, to represent their affairs in Parliament; but it is almost as difficult for the Representative to please the people there, as it is for the one who writes in Gaelic to please his readers here; and I understand that the gentleman lost his seat in the house this year. It is a true gentleman with whom we conclude, and how could it be otherwise, the best of the Gaels, one John MacDonald of the Black Isle people, close to Inverness. He has a beautiful estate on the banks of this river, and one or two estates throughout the district as well, and long may he enjoy them in good health

He and his beautiful wife,
The modest, mild gentlewoman.

But while mentioning the Gaels, how could I name anyone else before my old friend, a big-hearted man, reserved in speech, Hugh Chisholm; a man from whom the stranger has often received hospitality and the hungry person a meal, and why not, when he has plenty,

"And the nobility with hearts overwhelmed with joy at his qualities,
And he so humble, humane, clannish, and hospitable,"

that knowledge of his warm welcome precedes him. If my labour comes to fruition, let this be taken from me as a token of the esteem I have for him, as an honourable man, as a good neighbour, and as a true Gael.

The emigrant will understand from this that Gaels abound in

Goderich; but that is not all I would like him to understand, but also that they are doing well there, and that it would not be a bad place for many more of them. Every type of food which the soil of the area produces is easy to harvest from the earth in sufficient quantity, and I do not think there is a better fishing ground in the country than Lake Huron. Herring is usually about six dollars a barrel there; flour about the same price – potatoes about five dollars a barrel, apples about the same price when they are available – oats about two shillings a measure (34 pounds) – barley three shillings (54) – rye three shillings (54) – wheat from three shillings to a dollar (60) – sugar from a groat to a shilling (1) – tea from three shillings to a dollar – tobacco from nine pence to two shillings; there is plenty of this nasty substance growing there, but they do not prepare it as they do in Britain, but I would think, even so, that the taste could not be much worse in one place than it is in the other. Pork is five dollars (100) – beef four dollars – mutton is very rare – eggs from a groat to a shilling a dozen, but eighteen pence in the winter – fed birds from two shillings to four dollars a head – butter from eight pence to a shilling (1 pound) – cheese from six to ten pence (1).

Perishable and non perishable goods are more expensive here than anywhere else in the district. The reason for this greater expense is because it enjoys the highest elevation of any town in the district.

XII

OPINIONS ON AMERICA, &C.

❧

I have now guided the emigrant on a long, meandering journey through the country, but although I have, I know I have not done everything that he wants, and that he will say to me, "since you have gone the span, go the inch," since you have guided us to the country, tell us where we should make our home; but the Reader may remember that I did not undertake to do this at the outset of my small book, and indeed, it is one of the last things I should want to feel obliged to do. But while I did not promise to do this, I am so determined to give as much satisfaction as possible to my countrymen, that I will disclose my opinion to them on that matter as well: my opinion I say, for it is *my opinion* and not my advice that I will put forth, and I say openly that I am not seeking to inculcate or force that same opinion into anyone's head or heart, only insofar as his own examination, and the validity of the reasons I present, will open up a path for him.

For the head of the household, then, it is my opinion that Upper Canada is the best land that Britain has in America, and the particular districts that I would point out to him first above all, are the *Home District, London District,* or the *Huron Tract.* My most important reason for choosing Upper Canada as a country is that

JOHN GALT.

John Galt, from the Autobiography of John Galt. *London: Cockrane and McCrone, 1833.* Photography by Stratford Beacon Herald.

it has the best land, and the winter is not so long or quite so cold, as it is in Lower Canada, Nova Scotia, Cape Breton, &c. With the superiority of its land over the regions just named, a man living in Upper Canada can grow wheat, cucumbers, tobacco, and so forth, while those men cultivating the other regions will only have soft, slippery, little baby potatoes, and scant thirds of withered, hollow oats, that ripen in the summer frost, perhaps fourteen days before August. And my most important reason, for choosing the particular places I have pointed out, is that they have better land than the lower part of the country, and they are not so cold, that they have better land than the *Western District*, and they are not as unhealthy or as vulnerable to summer frost. But having said that, I would not want my readers to think that Upper Canada is a warm country in the winter; no, that is not at all what I mean; and any man who has never been away from Scotland may talk, read, imagine, and dream of cold until he goes gray, but as long as he lives, he will not comprehend the extent of the cold in Canada until he himself feels it or another cold equal to it. My ears have felt it, but though they have, I have no words to describe its harshness, as in truth, the Gaelic language is not capable of describing it, and since it is not, I have given up hope that there is any other language that can. But though neither I, nor my language, is able to impart even the least idea of its severity to my countrymen, nevertheless, since I once spent three *long* winters in the *sheltered* land of the Canada Company, I will undertake to tell you about each one of those winters. The first one lasted six months; that is, the snowy weather began on the twenty-seventh day of October, and on the twenty-seventh day of April, most of the land was visible – the second of these lasted exactly three months and seven days; that is, the snowy weather began on the first day of December, and on the second day of March, there was very little of it left – the third of these winters lasted five months and a few days; the snowy weather began around the first day of November and departed the first week of April. Now, though these winters were long as well as cold, none would come close how they were in the lower part of the country; and men who travel from Lower Canada and places like that, notice an improvement when they move, with regard to land and weather.

Employment for Labourers, or Farmers of Small Capital, Canada Company Poster, 1832. Courtesy of the J.J. Talman Regional Collection, D.B. Weldon Library, The University of Western Ontario. X2421.

But while it is clear to everyone who travels British America, that Upper Canada is its best region for the man who has a family, and who decides to make a permanent home for himself and for his descendants, I have always failed to see why it would be better than any other place in the country for a man who is interested

in earning a wage, and who is only striving to accumulate what-
ever small amount of money he can by the end of the year. There
are good wages to be found, no doubt, in parts of Upper Canada,
but even if there are, everything else is correspondingly costly,
and when they are compared, I would almost think that if a man
had a regular wage anywhere else in America, he would do as well
there as he would in Upper Canada. No doubt they do not retain
servants for long in places that have been only recently settled,
so if it is a sumptuous meal that a person needs, the advice I would
give him is to go over to the *Yankees*, for Canada does not come
close to the *States* in that regard. I believe that he would have little
reason to disparage the move in any way, for workers go over there
every single day of the year and receive a better wage than on our
side of the border. The labourer there receives the respect and
treatment of a gentleman. Even if his master is the great Sir
I--- M--- R---, he will sit at the same table, and he will not be
looked down upon because he is a poor man, as long as he is a
diligent, honourable man, who conducts himself well in his voca-
tion as a labourer, and who conducts himself beyond reproach
with respect to the general good of the country in which he and
his family settle, and above all, who makes himself useful to the
person who employs him. And the *States* are not only suitable for
labourers; when I consider all the opportunities there are on both
sides, I am compelled to take the opinion that some of the *States*
are better than any piece of Britain's possessions for a clever,
knowledgeable man, who has a good amount of money to start
out with. The *State of Ohio* and parts of the *State of Michigan* are,
without any doubt, the most suitable districts for a Briton, with
regard to purchasing land, between the two ends of America; and
it is easier to purchase land there than it is in the Queen's possessions. Canadian land is sold for as much as a dollar and three
quarters, while the States' land is only a dollar and a quarter. And
the *Yankees* give another advantage to a man with respect to pur-

chasing land, that is, if he pays one fifth the value of the land when he takes possession of it, he will receive a five year credit to pay the rest in five installments, an installment with interest at the end of each year. At this point I must note that the Canada Company follows this system, but the method by which the Queen's land[34] is acquired is as follows, five pounds of the value payable at once, and the rest of the sum eight days from that day, or the Queen's businessmen will have the land back and the five pounds along with it, and the emigrant will end up looking for his shoes. Any impartial man who looks at the two countries cannot deny that the States are progressing with incredible speed in comparison to Canada, for I could name villages there which were established in the same year as the Company's *towns*, from which there are three railways leaving today, and in which there are two newspapers, as well as local reports printed each week. A man who purchased a place in such a neighbourhood twelve years ago for a crown an acre, can sell it now for seven pounds, or perhaps twelve pounds an acre, so that the value of his land has increased while his money is lying in it. And what is the reason for that, except for the large number of emigrants who are going there, and if their few close friends still living among the Gaels were to get their wish, and succeeded in the cause people have been advocating for them, and a cause, I hope, they will continue to advocate for them[35], Canada would be brought to life and become a jewel for Britain, an honour to the supporters of the Gaels, and a comfortable, warm, and prosperous home for the emigrant. In order to bring about this situation, every poor Gael between the River Clyde and John O'Groat's house ought to raise a common shout in the ears of the supreme rulers of the Kingdom, to get free passage over and free land when they arrive, and I would not ask for more, since any man for whom that will not suffice is not worth bringing out from his fireside. Let them raise this plaintive cry, then, and may they not worry that it will not be understood, for a soft, gentle breeze from the wholesome mountain gusts will carry it, unadulterated, through every peril, mire, and storm, until, finally, it rings boldly and cheerfully in *Victoria*'s right ear. Let them send no one to parliament and I would almost say, to the pulpit, unless he is in favour of free emigration and giving free land to the people, and let them neither rest nor be silent until they get to a country that needs them, and to a country of which they have need, and let them leave "the old men wearing breeks," the dogs, and the renowned sheep,[36] basking in the sun on the face of the hillsides.

XIII

ON CHOOSING LAND, &C.

❧

When planning for this important business, we should not perform the trick of the English writers, who go over to America and run through the country like a clucking hen on a hot griddle, and who then come back and shout at the top of their voices that the choicest land in America is where the forest grows the thickest. If it were actually like this, it would save me no small trouble and you much of your labour; but since it is not, I will not complain about all my personal difficulties if I can only lessen your labours. But rather than being on the best land, the heaviest forest is actually most often on the worst land; I would not say that it was the worst ground if there were a means of making use of it, but what good is it for you, or me, for that matter, when the day will never come in which we will be able to get even the value of a single cuddy from it? The roughest forest I, or any other man, I think, have seen in America was actually growing on lifeless, low land, on which a man could be working ten years, before he would get out of it the value of what he might eat in only one of those years. In particular, there is an extremely heavy oak very often on this type of land, along with various types of pine and cedar - soft sugar, yellow birch, and swamp elm; woods I would advise men to avoid by all means, particularly if all the types I have named are growing close together. Let the emigrant choose the land on which he sees the following types of hardwood: - sugar-tree, beech-tree, white ash, black elm, red elm, viscous elm, walnut, butternut, hollow-tree, and cherry tree. If a person finds all of the varieties I have listed, growing amongst each other on a patch of level, dry land, and if all the other advantages are present, he cannot be far wrong; nevertheless, I would prefer that the sugar-tree be the most plentiful, and that the trees be tall, untangled, and straight, with juicy, tender branches, and robust, soft leaves. If a man finds a forest like this, it is a better indicator of the quality of the land than if the forest is rough (although it can sometimes be rough, and even very rough where it is like this); and the rougher and more crustaceous the bark appears on the sugar-tree, the better the indicator, but the thinner and greener it is on the *beech*, the better it is in that case. Where all the types of wood I have named are found growing amongst each other, the trees should usually be from fifty to sixty feet from the base to the lowest branches, particularly the elm, white ash, and hollow-tree; three varieties that are very useful for fences. Where all of these are found, the forest-floor[37] should be very sparse as well. But although the good land can be recognized by this method, there is another method by which it can be recognized as well: - trees are always going down in storms throughout the forest, and if a person looks for a place where this has happened, he will see what sort of land is there with his own two eyes, without being obliged to have any other man tell him. It would be wise for the emigrant to see whether there is good water on the land he is purchasing; if there is not enough water to challenge the summer drought and the winter frost, he will not get much satisfaction out of it. He must take care, all the same, that there are high, dry hills on it, close to the water, where he can build a house and cellar, and let him do his utmost to be close to a highway, a town, and, above all else, a mill.

XIV

ON CLEARING LAND, &C.

❧

Some Gaels expect that clearing land in America will be exceedingly arduous labour, and others expect that it will not be at all
difficult. Is it surprising, then, that one of these groups must be
mistaken? For clearing land in America is very painful work, that
is to say, if it is not done properly; and, on the other hand, it is
not too difficult for the man who knows how to do it correctly.
The emigrant will not know about it when he arrives, and how
could he? this is something he has never attempted; and something which he has never seen being attempted. But if he himself
does not know about it, there are many knowledgeable people who
will be prepared to assist him with advice when he begins that
work; twelve men and each man has his own advice. Since too much
"confusion, chit-chat, and idle words can drive one to distraction,"
I will offer my own advice before the others gather around.

Let the emigrant take my *advice*, and may he not heed any other
advice until he sees whether what I am proposing is suitable, that
is, that he clear the forest-floor before the foliage drops in the
fall, and gather it up in neat, tidy piles, and let him remember
my *advice* and cut it bare enough. If it is not cut with its foliage,
it will not be easy to kindle a fire in it, and if it is not cut bare,

Two Shanties on the Coldwater Road, Orillia Township, Ontario, September 1844, Titus Hibbert Ware. Courtesy of the Metropolitan Toronto Reference Library. T14381.

it will overtake everything that comes in its path, and it will have to be cut a second time. When a man begins to fell the great forest, he should remember that felling trees is only the easy part of the matter, that the greater part of the work consists of heaping them up together, and, therefore, he should always plan ahead. A man should always see if he can fell three or four of them beside each other, if possible, so that he does not have to do extra cutting or manoeuvering; for all those not felled in this way must be cut in fourteen or fifteen foot lengths, and dragged to the same place by oxen. People can see from this that the trouble of cutting them and heaping them up can be saved, to a great measure, if they are felled correctly. And they should look out for other difficulties, not just getting the stumps right. They must consider at the same time how to get the branches also; for if the top branches are not lopped off smoothly with an axe, and if they are not properly arranged close together, this will be as difficult to carry out as anything else. If a man wishes to fell the tree to the south, let him begin cutting on the south side first and cut well through its middle, and then let him go to the north side and continue cutting into it a little higher, and thus, if he is skillful, he will manage to set it down on the side he wishes. He should fell all of the largest trees first, if they are not suitable to split for fences; but if they are, the best way is to leave them standing till the end. Fence wood must be cut as close as possible to twelve feet, so that it will be easier to split, and more suitable for fencing. They split these four inches thick; and they usually receive a half dollar per hundred for this work. It costs from six to nine dollars to have an acre of forest cut down, and about as much again to burn and enclose it. The recent emigrant will necessarily be exceedingly awkward at all of this work, and since cutting in particular is dangerous work, he should be careful, especially when felling a tree, for, as soon as it parts from its stump, it may have the misfortune of getting caught up in one or two others, which it bends in front of it half way to the ground, and then, if they can, these others will spring back just as far again, showering twigs, chips, and branches all at once around him, as swiftly and as numerous as the quiver of arrows driven out of the "canvas bowstrings" around Don Quixote's helmet. I would recommend that anyone in this perilous situation should jump quickly behind another tree, for one tree is just as capable of protecting him as another is of killing him. A stranger to the axe is also terribly prone to hurting himself with it, at first. The "Guide" has seen those who have sent a piece of their shoe, along with their toes, to the other side of town with one swing. He has seen others stitching their shoe, their foot, and the tree together with an axe, until the axe was dragged out by force. In order to avoid all accidents of this nature, as much as possible, the emigrant should do everything very slowly, not rushing at all. He will learn best that way, and he will be more productive also, for hurry-scurry and hacking about will not accomplish the work in America at all. Let him remember that

it is neither today's and tomorrow's work, nor this year's and next
year's work, that he is commencing, but work that will not end
as long as he lives, and not only that, but which will be only half
finished when he dies. At any rate, that is not to say that he will
not become good at it; he certainly will, and the less he knows
about the work at first, the better it will be, for though some may
be surprised, it is quite certain that any man trained to use the
axe at home has not been, is not now, and will never be good at
it after going to America: he will be just like a young lad, who
has spent five years in a bad school, for it is easier to make a good
student of an infant who does not know his A, B, C, than it is
to remove even a portion of the bad, old ways from his head.
Winter is the best time by far for cutting. The hardwood is *softer*
at that time with the frost, and it is neither so tough nor so difficult to break apart, as it is in the summer. The weather is often
so *fresh* in the winter that the cutter will not be in *danger* of losing
much sweat over it. It will take from eight to twelve days to cut
an acre properly, for an expert, able worker; but an emigrant,
having recently left the old country, would need eighteen days to
learn it, and he would not have it right even after all that: using
an axe is dangerous work, and the best one to speak about it is
a "man who has made it his special trade."

A person need never attempt to burn the forest until the
warmth of spring has fully arrived, and until he thinks that
everything he sees is almost ready to catch fire on its own, if it
is not kindled by another means. Brushwood is the first thing
to which he tries to set fire, and if it is not dry enough, and
helped by a good gust of wind, it is cursed work: it is worse
than thirty hours of heath burning. No man engaged in this work
will have a single lock of hair or an eyebrow that is not scorched
as red as the mouth of a bellows. Once he has burned the forest-
floor, the next thing to which he sets his hands is heaping up
the great forest. This work requires four men and a yoke of oxen.

In a day, a crew of that size should be able to gather up an acre that has been felled and cut properly into thirty-five piles. But the most common method, if there are enough people and oxen in a neighbourhood, is to come together on one day, expressly for this sort of work. Every fifth man is responsible for working the oxen, and each one has his own particular crew to pile up the wood, once he brings it to them with the oxen. A man might suppose that this is quite enjoyable work, especially when he knows that there will be an extra man on the field. An extra man! but what will he be doing? This *willing worker!* He will go about as quickly as his feet can take him, shouting *"grog, grog,"* from morning to night, till he grows hoarse. He will have a large, full bucket of "murky pond water" in one hand, and another bucket, every bit as large, in the other hand, full of the *drink-of-Ferintosh*[38] – there will be a substantial drinking cup splashing on top of it, just like a small, six-oared galley at anchor in a Highland harbour, and every man will dip and raise it until the *"grog Boss"* is full – and take a swig from it – then he will hurry to wash his mouth out with the water, but accidents are just as likely to happen to a man there as they are anywhere else, and it is quite possible that he will take another cup of the same stuff. Every other convenience will be provided in a similar manner all day, but when night falls, a thing which is no small matter will occur. The brave men will eat their supper, and they will eat it heartily also, and it would be a pity if they did not, for it is often so good that they do not need to be called to it; more particularly, their arms, and their backs, tell them that they have truly earned it. Then the *sweet stuff* starts going around. Song is the next diversion to which they are compelled. Then another drink, and, little by little, they end up plucking out each other's eyes. This is often how they start and finish up when raising a building as well. But if the emigrant takes my *advice*, he will go home before they strike blows.

A Forest Home, W.H. Bartlett, in Willis' Canadian Scenery, *1848.*
Photography by Axel Menzefricke.

To return to my main point, when the wood has been stacked, the top of each pile is set afire and kept alight till the last shaving is spent. Then a person must rake up every little stick, shaving, and leaf on the ground into heaps, and set them on fire along with the rest; and he must take every precaution to ensure that the ashes are scattered before water gets on them; for if their essence is washed out of them, not much will grow, for that year, in the place where they are burned,. When every job I have mentioned is finished, a person will have no reason to delay from sowing the land, but even as he constructs a fence around it, three feet of each stump will remain in the field, to bear witness to "the farmer's diligent handiwork."

XV

ON CROPS, &C.

Once the land in America is prepared up to the point at which we left it in the last chapter, the farmer can plant any seed which is used in that country. If he plants wheat, eight gallons (sixty pounds) will be enough for an acre; but if he is planting oats, an acre requires almost sixteen gallons (68) of seed. They usually plant oats from the beginning of May till the end of June, and the oats will always be ripe three to four months after that; but they have two types of wheat – that is, a type which they plant in the spring, and another which they usually plant in the fall. They plant the fall wheat, whenever they can obtain it, from the first of August until the snowy weather stops them; but September is the best time. If it is planted earlier than that, it will be in danger of rotting under the snow in winter; and if it is later, it will be in danger of dying with the frost, before the snow covers it, and after the snow leaves. The wheat which is planted like this, in mid-fall, should be ready for the sickle by the following July, if the year is favourable. But the spring wheat will take only about three months in the earth between sowing and reaping. Whichever type of wheat, or of any other type of seed a man plants there, except Indian corn and potatoes, all he needs to do is to sow the seed on top of the soil and harrow it; and some knowledgeable men say that it should not be harrowed too much. I cannot offer the reader any opinion as to how much produce he may look forward to per acre, either from the fall wheat or the spring wheat. Sometimes it is close to forty pecks of seed, and other times ten pecks; but at any rate, I know that where there is a good crop of the fall wheat, it is far superior to the spring variety, and, if it is planted at the right time, in fresh soil, with the right seed, it should not be less than twenty pecks. The most useful and successful crops a farmer can plant in Canada are found where the wheat grows well.

They plant Indian corn and potatoes in the same fashion in America, using fresh soil. They take a hoe and lift a handful of earth; they throw in two or three clusters of seed, and they let the earth fall back on top; and so on, approximately two feet apart from each other, till they have covered the field. When the crop appears a few inches out of the ground, they cultivate it again and lift the soil around it; and a man need not bother with it again until he lifts it into the pot. But other people make a single job of it – that is, they lift the soil around the crop when they plant it; and they do not look at it again until the desire for potatoes, or hunger, sends them to see if there is anything underneath. The most suitable time to plant potatoes in Upper Canada is from the end of April to the twenty-fifth day of June; and if the year is suitable for planting good seed, a barrel of seed may yield forty barrels. Nevertheless, I would not want the emigrant to think he could expect that every year; but I imagine, however, that it would rarely be under twenty barrels, especially if he gets the yield he should. The one thing that most weighs against potatoes in America is the difficulty experienced protecting them from frost in the winter. If a person puts them in a cellar, they are exceedingly likely to rot in one way or another; and if he puts them in a pit, it is excessively difficult to preserve them as well.

If the frost comes before the snow falls at the beginning of winter, it will touch them. Similarly, if the frost comes in the spring after the snow melts, it will touch them. If a person puts a great deal of earth on top, and very heavy snow lies on top of them as well, they will heat up and rot. If he puts only a little earth on top, and the snow does not cover them, they will not be able to escape either. Thus, it is a difficult, and entirely uncertain matter. Nonetheless, if they can be saved at all, they are a very useful crop in a new country; for a man need go neither to a kiln nor to a mill with them.

They plant Indian corn, or the great barley, as the Gaels call it in America, at the beginning of June. There is no grain as susceptible to the cold as this is at first. The slightest frozen moisture will completely destroy it. And it needs to soak up the warmth, not only at the beginning, but at every moment till it is fully ripe. Light, sandy soil, and a hot sunny exposure are best suited to it. It does not require any manure; and neither, in my opinion, would it need to see a drop of rain from the day it goes into the ground until the day it comes out. Just as quickly as it appears out of the ground, it continues to grow; and it grows indeed. Its tender leaves are softer and more succulent than July cabbage, and its colour is much deeper and more robust than watercress. If the weather is so hot that the midday sun forces it to droop, that is what suits it best. It will perk up its ears in the late afternoon, and it stretches up wonderfully, so that it often reaches fourteen, fifteen, and sometimes sixteen feet high. Though the ear of corn is exceedingly heavy, the stalk is correspondingly hardy, so that it stands straight on its base, something like a young pine tree. When it approaches its full height, the method they have for harvesting it is to stand in saddles on horseback and to cut the ear off around its base; but it is not often so tall in Canada that those afoot cannot do the job: the "Guide" actually saw horsemen doing this in the States. As long as its straw is green, it is suitable for livestock. Indeed, I do not believe that anything else grows in the earth that is better than it, in that respect; and its seed is very good for cattle also, but it does not taste pleasant to people who are not accustomed to it. Pea meal is the closest thing to it that I know of.

Peas are a crop that responds very well in Canada. Though the straw is not good for livestock, peas produce a great quantity of seed; and the seed is wonderfully useful for feeding swine – a type of animal that cannot at all be dispensed with in the new country. The only possible skill to practise with peas there is to plant early, and not to plant too thickly, and to be certain that they are harvested before they get too ripe, else the sowing seed and all the rest will be lost in a single day, because of the way they open up in the heat of the sun. They are easier to dry over there than people here have experienced; and, as for harvesting, a baby could do it.

A First Settlement, W.H. Bartlett, in Willis' Canadian Scenery, *1848.*
Photography by Axel Menzefricke.

As for garden crops, they grow without any problems in the fields of Canada, especially in earth that has been freshly cleared. They have a great number of varieties there of which I had never heard until I saw them; and I would not be able to recount all of them here, even if I tried; but I know there are many, even among the Gaels, who bestow more of their attention and their time to these things than they ought. I do not mean carrots, onions, and so on, are not good in their own place; but, despite that, it is a poor business to be investing labour on them that should be spent clearing land and doing other useful things of that sort. Stumbling awkwardly around gardens, around fruits, making sugar and other trifles, is the most wasteful and most foolish work a family which has newly emigrated can set its hand to. It is by fumbling around in this manner, that hundreds keep themselves in poverty from year to year, always forgetting there is a crop to harvest, until the time comes when the other half needs to be planted. Then they will not have any fresh land cleared; and they will have to begin ploughing and harrowing the same area from which they harvested last year the very seed, as it were, they are planting this year. That work takes as much time as it did to clear the land in the first place, and the third crop they should have had will not be harvested either. But the man who clears a patch of land every year will not only have a good crop, but the value of his land will increase also; for there is not an acre that is not worth four pounds more cleared than it is wild; and, moreover, what grows on it will be his, as long as he lives. In order to follow this plan, men would need to let a portion of land lie fallow every year, in order to allow more land to be brought under cultivation; and a man should, by all means, plant grass on it before taking more than two crops from the soil, so that, at the least, he has it cleared. The grass is very useful for livestock; and it keeps the land strong and in good order, without going wild with plants – something to which American soil is very prone.

By paying close attention to the system I have described, a man and his animals will have plenty from one end of the year to the other end. He will have winter feed for cattle and horses — he will have summer grazing for sheep, and food for pigs, without need, want, or poverty — he will have the appearance of prosperity, his family will appear well fed, and everything around him will have the look of success; meanwhile another man will be tormented in the midst of poverty, without possessions, without credit, without respect — bailiffs and their dogs biting at his ears - and, to make a long story short, he will be forever falling into mischief.

XVI

ON GRASS, &C.

If you want to harvest *grass* from the land you have cleared by
yourself in America, do not think ill of me for reminding you
that you will need to plant it first; for though you allowed it to
grow, after clearing the land to your satisfaction, not a single
blade of grass would come up through the earth: and I will tell
you why. Though the forests of America are famous for how well
they support livestock, this does not happen with natural grass,
as we call it, but with many varieties of plants that are both
exceedingly succulent and noted for their growth, and preferably
both, all summer long. Each variety of these plants has its own
innate system, as it were; for one type leaves and another arrives
without me (or anyone else, I expect) knowing why. As few of
them blossom, they wither away in a moment, and, in a shorter
time than you can imagine, there will be another type covering
all the area where the one that has just departed used to be. In
remote areas, where there are not many cattle to destroy them,
they are a very pleasant sight. If the forest is somewhat sparse,
and the land round about is somewhat level, they are indeed a
truly beautiful sight, all of them at the same height, as if one has
made an agreement with the other not to go an inch past it, either

this way or that way. But while the plants in one area are about the same height, and plants in another area are also of equivalent heights, nevertheless, all plants are not the same height everywhere, for in some places, they reach the knee, in other places the calf, in other places the ankle, and so forth. The *Wild Onion*[39] is the first one of these plentiful families to appear. Once Shrovetide arrives, it keeps watch day and night, as it were, to see when it might welcome the cattle to the forest for their breakfast, the very cattle who have been crouching up against the walls, and who have no hope of finding anything to eat outside the stall. It would be a most substantial, powerful meal, strengthening the cattle. No doubt, they will not take long to devour it, and certainly, they should make good use of it in May, for by June, who can say, "This is where the *Onions* were"? It is the first to arrive, and the last to leave; if the bard had settled in America, when could he imagine or sing of the primrose?

You will clothe yourself in spring,
And the rest will hide their eyes.

But if the *Onion* departs, as it must, it does not go without leaving a memorial behind, as long as a piece of spring butter or cheese remains. You will understand this is not a very pleasant memorial, when I tell you no man can permit an animal who feeds on it, to brush up against him, because of its absolutely putrid breath, after it eats the *Onions*. This virtue (if I may call it a virtue) of the *Onion*, spreads through the pores of the whole animal, so that the meat cut from it, the milk milked from it, the butter and cheese made from that same milk, and not only that, but the pork prepared with May buttermilk and whey, will be, to a certain extent, as sour as garlic. No person unaccustomed to it can partake with pleasure of any of these things I have mentioned. But why do I need to say that? Cannot a people who chew tobacco as ably as the Gaels of today, eat anything?

If the *Onion* is sour and has an unpleasant odour, that is not the case for the plant that follows it, *Cattle Cabbage* — a worthy plant that would not displease any person while he remained without potatoes or spring wheat. This is a soft, bushy, low-lying plant, a little like our own *silverweed* in appearance, but completely different in nature. It is very good feed for animals, and men eat it also, after cooking it along with meat, just as we prepare cabbage here. I remember getting it one day for dinner in the house of a gentleman who had come out from Edinburgh, and who lived, at that time (and still does, if I am correct), on the shore of Lake Huron, a few miles from Goderich; and, it was very good indeed. The *Cattle Cabbage* is longer lived than the Onion, and it deserves to be, for it is an exceedingly useful plant; no animal alive will want for anything so long as it remains, and when it runs out, nothing else as good will follow it, from what I have seen.

My task will not permit me to give you a description of each individual plant, and since it will not, I will pass over them without mentioning any more, no further than to note that they are so plentiful and so close together in the forest, that neither *grass* nor grain can grow there, only plants and young saplings of many varieties of trees you have never seen, and perhaps never will. But do not suppose, for all that, that it is the plants which keep the grass out of the forest. It is not those at all; they would hardly be capable of it. What keeps it out is that the grass has no parent there, and even if it did, it could not grow amongst the foliage, and above all else, in the shade of the trees. From this, you can see there is neither root nor seed cast from it into the ground, and therefore, you need not expect to see it until you plant it; but if you plant in the manner, and at the time we directed you, you will have a good crop of it, even though every other grain were to forsake you for a season; nonetheless, do not promise yourself that you will have five or six tons an acre, as some of the English Writers maintain: two Tons an acre is not a bad crop in that part of the world.

The *hay-grass* should be tended to early in America, so that it covers the ground before the weather becomes too hot, for if it is eaten bare at the beginning of the summer, the heat of the sun is so great that it will burn up, and it will not be any good for the rest of the year. Thus, if tended to at the right time, the grass can be cut around the eighth, or at the latest, the twelfth day of July, and if the weather is suitable at that time for the work, the grass that is cut today, as it were, can be planted again tomorrow. The Americans say its moisture is none the worse for taking a little of the sun's heat, but the smallest shower of rain, or sometimes too much sun, will destroy it; and every man who knows about farming, knows that grass that is not left out to dry as it should is worth little. If it is made into stacks, they should be thatched over quickly, for the rain often comes down very heavily about this time, and the weather is always so calm and warm afterwards, that all of the hay or grain that it has poured on will rot in a minute. But I need not say much more about this matter; if the "emigrant" winters a few cattle the first year, the "guide" will warrant that he will be careful enough with his hay the next year without any more warning than the natural elements themselves will give him.

Before we leave this subject, it will be wise for me to tell you that fine, natural grass grows on low pools beside rivers in many places in America, and tough, strong grass, of very little use, here and there throughout the forest, around hollows and marshes; but I would advise you to avoid these when you are choosing land upon which you may depend for crops.

One other word and we will start another topic. As long as you can grow two tons of grass an acre, and the nature of the American winter remains unchanged, I think that grass is the most useful grain you can plant.

XVII

ON THE MAKING OF SUGAR

❧

The Sugar Camp is what the people of America call the place where they engage in this amazing work, and any person wanting to set up the camp properly would need to see to his affairs long, long before it is time to begin. That is, he must mark out which spot is most suitable for it, with regard to forest and land; and then cut the forest-floor as low to the ground as possible and gather it up neatly out of the way of man and beast. All of this must be done as early as the beginning of winter, before the snow lies too deep, for then there will be no way to cut it correctly.

The next thing he should set his hand to is getting suitable pots, and carving out Troughs to collect the sap. These should be made of Black Ash, for it is a wood that will ruin neither the taste nor the colour; and another of its notable characteristics is that it is not likely to split in the sun. It would also be useful to have enough firewood on site, cut – split – heaped up, early in the season. Then, when the Spring finally arrives, and you see a hint of the thaw on everything, set out for the "Camp" – take an axe or auger – put a gash in the south side of each tree that you intend to use in this business – make a notch with a gouge under the gash – drive a spile into the notch, and place a trough below at the base of the tree to collect the sap as it runs down the spile. Have the pots prepared now, kindle the fire – tend to it, and stand by it. Send the boys away with containers to transport the sap to you – pour it in the pots – bring it to a vigorous boil, and you will see, in a short while, that it will turn a deep brown colour, though in its natural state, it was just as clear as, and, without a doubt, much cleaner than the Drink-of-Ferintosh – increase the boil: for the greater the steam, the better it is – Taste now, if you wish, the fruits of your labour. See how sweet it is! Very good, "patience makes good fishing," continue – Taste it again. It is now a dark russet colour, and sweeter than anything you have ever tasted, your lips even sticking together with it – it has now become much thicker, with a very great steam rising from it. If this is the case, lower the fire and be careful – take a pot-stick and stir it about, so that it does not scorch; and as soon as it comes to a "porridge boil," you must be very careful with it. It will be advisable about this time, to put a jug of milk or a clot of blood into it, to purify it. No sooner does it boil after putting this in, than all the sediment and impurities rise to the top, so that these dregs can be thrown out, without losing any of the Sugar. A little more simmering and it can be removed from the fire. If you wish to make Granulated Sugar from it, continue stirring until it cools; but if you wish to make Loaves, you must have containers at hand in which to pour it, just like your porridge-pot. When it has cooled in the containers, turn them upside down, and shake it out, as a housewife usually does with the cheese vat when taking the cheese out of it.

You know yourself that sugar is such a sweet thing that men do not want to leave it without dipping their fingers into it. I think this is enough of an excuse for me to stay with it just now, at least until I can tell you what to do with it after you transport it home. If you intend to put it into a chest or a barrel to keep it from the children and the servant (often something very difficult to do, for pilferers are just as clever in America as they are in Scotland), be careful not to leave it long in a cold, damp place, or it will become moist and melt away. Neither should you set it in a very hot place close to the hearth, or it will melt there also. It likes the middling state, for much like us, it cannot withstand extremes of either cold or heat.

XVIII

ON LIVESTOCK

❧

Horses.

It would be no wonder if, in any way, America were still behind
the old country with regard to livestock. But though this is true
in some respects, it is not in other respects. There is not one man
among the English Writers, who has seen the horses of America,
that is, no man who knew the needs of a horse, the superiority
of a horse, and the beauty of a horse, who has not willingly com-
plimented them, for they are superior to what he has seen before,
and better than what he expected to see. But though the horses
are a novelty for them, because of how clever and hardy they are,
they need not be so for the Gael, particularly when he sees they
are no different from the Scottish stud he left behind on the hill
of springs. They are truly good horses, and fully affirm the truth
of the proverb which says,

"The good horse commends himself."

When I saw them, I understood how much harm the Gaels

did when they mixed the best of their own stud with the slow, clumsy horses which they were getting from the south. The large horses are more suitable, without a doubt, around port towns where heavy loads are placed on them, while, at the same time, the mob is so thick in front of their noses that no one can move more quickly than anyone else; but who can depend on them through rugged country, boggy land, and hillsides? Canadians today are as eager as can be to ruin their own horses in the same way, taking over the big, splay-footed horses from England to improve their breed, or so they hope, without at all remembering it is said that "the fool's head is often big." But the foreign variety has not yet been spread throughout the entire country. Not many of them are seen in Upper Canada, and neither do the French in Lower Canada have many; except the one type of gelding, the best behaved and the smartest there could be. I need not describe them. There is not a shade of difference between them and the Highland horses, except that they are a bit more pointed in the nose and somewhat leaner and firmer in the legs, and I think all of that could be derived from the dry climate of the country in which they are raised. My reason for thinking this is that I do not know of any island, valley, or district of wet land in Scotland or America, whose inhabitants, be they man or beast, are not broader, clumsier, and softer in the ankles, and broader and more snoutish in the nose than their neighbours dwelling on dry land. And if it does that to those at home, it is not strange that it should do the same to horses in Canada:

"For the heather is not their pasture,
Neither the moors at the top of the mountains."

The horses which the Indians always use up on the *St. Clair* are altogether too small; they are not more than an inch taller than the small horses on Uist; but the country people's horses are approximately fourteen hands high. They are not used for working a cart with one of them in a halter; in fact, the country people use a pair of them together in a four-wheeled waggon with one slender stick, which they call a *tongue* coming up between them from the waggon, tied to their bridles. As soon as the equipage is placed on them, and they get the slightest encouragement, they tear off at an impetuous trot, and they will not look at anything or anyone, but will head straight out, to put behind them everything that lies before them. They do not care whether the ground is soft or hard, wet or dry; whether they go up or down hill, they will not rest a muscle unless the waggoner compels them to slow down. Even were they to attempt to go slowly, as the horses here do, they would not know how, for they were trained first to trot, and they do not know how to change. But although their movement is really very good, and in fact the best, on black, loamy soil, they are not entirely objects of wonder because of the way they travel, until the winter snow comes. The people have a type of sledge which they put on them at that time, and because the sledges are so easy to pull on the snow, the horses can travel such a distance that a man can scarcely believe it, unless he has guessed at the superior strength of the geldings. I knew of them doing sixty miles a day, from time to time, in my own neighbourhood, and that was despite a shortage of feed. And I have seen some of them going that distance under saddle, even when the roads were bad in the spring, and heavy, *fleshy* people riding them. It will be appropriate for me to note here that the people go on small trips several times in the winter, with only one horse, in a small, low vehicle they call a *cutter*. If the emigrant has had any instruction in this matter, he should try to obtain a little filly, along with one of these cutters, within a year or two after arriving; for it will save him a great deal of time with how quickly it makes the trip to the market, the smithy, the mill, and so forth, and time is the most precious thing a new farmer has there.

Everyone knows that one horse is as difficult to winter there as a yoke of oxen, but although it is, if the emigrant takes my advice, and plants grass early in the season, he will have enough hay to take a horse through the winter in a short time; and, in addition to the use the horse will have from it, he can be raising other animals with it. If he wishes to have a horse for himself, and a horse to spare when it is requested, let him plant grass in due time: grass, grass, above all else; as for the man who decides not to plant grass seed in due season, let him not go to America. A good farm horse costs from fifty to four hundred dollars in Canada. A five year old mare, as good a horse as a person could ever ask to see, can be obtained for eighty to a hundred dollars. Many times, people will buy a good, solid beast from the Indians around the *St. Clair*, for twenty dollars, or perhaps fifteen, if the Indians need money; but these will be neither domesticated nor trained, but will be just as wild as a year-old roe. A smith in Canada will take four dollars for making a set of shoes, and putting them on a horse. A Highland farmer will think that is much too expensive, and it is indeed expensive, but thereafter, it will take less money to keep shoes on a horse in Canada than in the Highlands. The reason for that is how free the land is from stones, and how long-lasting the winter snows are; for the same shoes will do from Hallowtide to May Day, if they are adjusted on their hoofs, from time to time. Halters are very costly there, but that cannot be helped: the type they have here would not be suitable, even if they were taken over.

Cattle.

If the horses of America are similar to Highland horses, that is not the case with cattle. Their two ancestors were only distantly related. Theirs are long-legged, smooth, lean — with slender thighs, and they are open from the crotch, almost to the haunch.

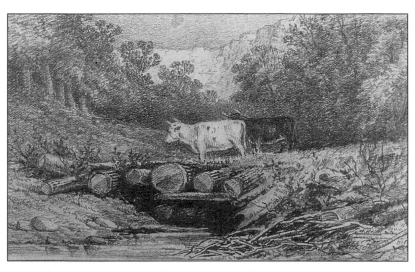

Log Bridge near Owen Sound (Derby Township, Ontario), August 1874), George Harlow White. Courtesy of the J. Ross Robertson Collection, Metropolitan Toronto Reference Library. T16503.

They have long, narrow, elegant necks; but I maintain that their noses are every bit as long; and their mid-sections are just as short. But regardless of that: they grow nicely when they get a good opportunity; and an exceedingly good yield of milk is given by the type of cow there. If I ignore the colour black, there is no other colour that they do not have, and twelve other colours, I think, that I have not seen before; but a person could travel two hundred miles before he saw one head that was completely black — that is, of the four-footed variety. As for men, black-haired ones can be found in plenty in Canada. Since the cattle there are free to roam through the forest all summer, the heifers usually have their calves in their second year; and this greatly deforms them. In addition to ruining their growth, it ruins their shape, and especially their horns; for while a person can see the most hand-some horns he could ever wish to see on oxen, he will find only small, white, stunted horns, about the size of snuff horns, on the milk cows. I also imagine they would be much better for milk, were it not for that; for it is natural to think that what leaves them wanting in the one instance will do likewise in the other. A milk cow there costs from fifteen dollars to twenty dollars at the beginning of winter; but the cow that costs that much at the beginning of winter cannot be bought for less than twenty-five to thirty dollars at the end of spring. A small heifer in calf can be purchased, perhaps, for fifteen, even in the spring; but a person should not expect that she will be of much use to his family that year. A man cannot get a team of oxen that is fully trained, and mighty in strength, for under sixty dollars, and he need not expect the best for less than eighty; but a team of decent three-year-olds, untrained, can be purchased for fifty-five; two-year-olds, from thirty to forty; yearlings, from fourteen to twenty-four; and calves, from ten to fifteen a pair. But though the emigrant could get every type I named at half-price, he ought not to be rash in buying them for a year or two in the beginning. Wintering livestock in Canada is a distressing business, and losing them in spring is the most vexing thing that can happen to a person. I knew of scores who lost their labour, their time, and their possessions, in this way - envious men, who with little money starting out, struggled to satisfy their haughty ambitions, and to have more than their neighbours; but, instead, they actually failed in both and were in danger of being worse than penniless. But the best method for the man who wishes to succeed in this business is to purchase a few at first, and be good to them, and it will not be long until they multiply. A person should understand that the forest is a good habitat for them in the summer, when the two-year-olds have calves; and though the winter snowstorms rage, if there are only a few of them, the cattle would not be terribly difficult to maintain, given their robust condition around November. They enjoy the shade of the trees; but the woodcutter must take care that an animal does not come under the tree that he is felling. The "Guide" has seen their marrow and their brains being mashed on the snow because of lack of attention to this. Raising cattle there, in one way, is just like it is in the Highlands. In the case of the man who keeps a few of them, and who has plenty for them, they will breed in a short while; but the man who keeps more than he should, given what he has to provide them with, will make more on hides than he will on meat. Lean cattle are liable to twenty diseases in Canada, and I dare say, more than that. There is a disease of the horns. This occurs so close to the brain that it is no laughing matter, right in the core of the horn — where no man will notice it, until he sees a bad look on the animal suffering with it. And often it can progress from here, before people who do not know about it notice it; and even if they do know about it, if they have not been wise and very observant of the ways of cattle from their youth, it can trick them. When do you think the little, pale weaver who goes over from Glasgow would suspect there was anything wrong with his cow, as long as he could see nothing wrong with her, from the outside of her horn? But what the emigrant ought to do, if he has any doubt about the cow, is to take hold of her horn; and if the disease is in that horn, he will find it to be, to some extent, just as hot as a potato he picks out of the pot, when it is at full boil. If it is like this, he should throw her onto her back, and bore a hole at the base of the horn with a strong gimlet. Then he should let her back on her feet, and the pus inside will drip out of the hole. Then let him put her back onto the ground; and take a cupful of fine salt and well-ground spice, and blow it into the horn through the shaft of a quill. He should do this as quickly as he can, and secure it with a rag, opening it at the end of every week for a month, and nothing can compare to it. Cattle there are susceptible to another disease, which they call the "tail-disease." This originates in the tail, in the same manner as the other begins in the horn; and if it is not stopped soon enough, not only will it consume the tail, but it will finish the body as well. The best way to cure this is to make a split in the hide, and knead the things I mentioned previously into a little pig fat, and put a portion of that mixture inside; but if a large portion of the tail is like an empty husk, because of the extent to which the disease has progressed in it, the most certain method is to take a black-dagger40, and sever the tail from the body.

This will suffice to let the emigrant see that cattle are susceptible to many diseases in the new country, just as in other places; and I do not expect that this is any cause for wonder in a place where livestock stay out, in many instances, from Hallowtide to May Day, with only the remains of the fodder they get in the evening between them and the snow. The people of the Highlands think that an animal cannot be wintered outside in Canada; but this is not so. In new areas, they actually confine almost none of them. Over there, cattle will stay at the edge of the forest which is closest to the house, every animal having gone into its own bed in a round hollow; and from there it will not stir until morning. When it moves, the snow will melt under it, and around it, and it will let out a cry that would make a coward tremble. There will be icicles hanging from its nose, and a mantle of the same hard snow covering its back and its whole body. It will let out a sigh, and shake itself; but when it shakes, it shakes in earnest! — some of the great sheet of ice will leave its back, and the ice will fall from its nose, and blood will follow. But though there will be blood, it will not be in danger of losing much: before you can count to seven, the blood will be as hard as any other part of the nose. And is it not a cause for wonder that cattle should grow in Canada after all this? and not only that, but that they should also grow well. The person writing this was aware of a four-year-old ox which was killed and eaten, in the *Huron Tract*, which had never been through a door, and did not get enough straw to make a hen's nest for the first two years; but, after every hardship it came through, it weighed one thousand

and seven pounds — that is, between fat, flesh, and leather. But if the brave ox got neither a blade of grass nor one of straw, there were many juicy top branches of the sugar-tree, and a good dishful of salt that went into its gullet; it is true they give salt to live-stock in Canada. They give salt to every type of livestock, except the pigs. They always give it to the horses once a week; and to the cattle and sheep twice a week. A cow gets approximately a porridge-spoon full, and a sheep gets approximately a *tea*-spoon full. Canadian cattle are so keen on salt, that if a person wants to see how many there are around him in the forest, all he needs to do is to stand on a high spot, and shout, *"Cow-salt, cow-salt, cow-salt"*; and they will gather around him as quickly as cats gather around the dairymaid when she calls, "Pussy, pussy, pussy," upon returning from the milking. It seems to me that cattle in partic-ular could not do without salt in the summer. The plants are so tender, and so moist and runny, that they would not be able to digest them, without something to bind and strengthen the stomach. But, on the other hand, I think that the horses and sheep, living on sown green grass, could do without it. Nevertheless, there is no doubt that all of them would be better off with it, not only there, but here as well; and if they were accustomed to it here, they would like it well enough also. Salt increases an animal's desire for food, and endows it with an appetite for eating everything that comes near it, and it is not hesitant to drink its fill — something that is always very good for an animal after getting fodder. At any rate, in Canada, they must have it, by all means, as long as they live; but once they are killed, not much is wasted on salt; for as soon as the entrails are taken out of the winter cow, the meat can always be stored until fourteen days after Shrovetide without putting an ounce of salt on it. This is very convenient, for salt is as high in price as seven dollars a barrel in parts of Canada; and since the meat stays fresh all winter, it is a great saving.

Reports on Cattle.

The cattle in America are of many colours, and is that any great wonder? and they have many different shapes, but who should be surprised at all that, given the number of countries and kingdoms from which they are driven? It would be a strange thing if the men were not of different colours and shapes in Canada, where some of them are from every kingdom I could name; and it would be no less amazing if the cattle were not the same, since they were transported there from various counties of England and Ireland, the Lowlands of Scotland, France, and from many other places, which my task will not permit me to name. This is all very well, but were they taken over from the best place; that is, was the most suitable kind for the country, in every sense, taken there? It was not, and will not be, until they drive over the "handsome herd," of the type the English speakers call "*West Highlanders.*" Of every species of cattle I have seen, there were none among them that would suit Canada as well as these. And I am not at all without support in this opinion; for there is not a farmer there, who knows the Highland cattle, and the good attributes naturally bred into them, who does not often lament that he does not have them; most particularly, in the depth of winter. The one thing that frightens some people about them is that the snow might impede them, because of the thickness of their coats, but the day will come when no one thinks this way, except for those who do not know about wintering Highland cattle outdoors. I will leave this as proof for every man who has considered it, and the man who has not done so, let him consider it now, and imagine he sees twenty head of cattle, of the right Highland variety, on a hillside on a day of snow and drifts, with one bare, lean, Foreign beast among them. I say, if he does see that; and if every head of the twenty is not active, lively, and in good health, without a snowflake above its houghs [hocks], and if the one chilled, feeble beast is not standing, cringing, with its back to the blast, and with a mantle of snow covering it from horn to tail, let him say that the Guide has no skill. Thus, it is easy to understand that the Highland cattle are better suited to North America than any other variety, for they would stand up better to the cold, they would be easier to feed, their meat and leather would be better, the oxen among them would be hardier and stronger for work, and they would travel much better on the road when going with seed to the mill, and so forth. They would go briskly and smartly through bushes and marshes in the forest, and the large cattle among them would be swift, fierce, and resolute in protecting the calves and yearlings from the bears and wolves: two types of wild animals which often cause great harm to cattle there. But those are only a few of the attributes which make them suitable for the country about which we are speaking, if we had space and time we could name more of them; but we do not have that, and since we do not, we will leave it. I know very well that some will say they are not good for milk, and as proof of that, they will point out to us those Lowland cattle that go north every summer and fall. That Lowland cattle go north, we admit, and that (in a way) more go there than ought to, we do not deny; but that Highland cattle are not very good for milk, we will neither believe nor admit. We are not saying that all Highland cattle are good for milk; but the proper sort are exceedingly good for it. And neither are we saying, that there will be as many good milk cows among the Highland cattle, as there are among the Lowland cattle, nor that they are as suitable for being near towns, where people sell milk for sixpence; but we will say that those cows they do have are so good, that there will be more cream, and extra butter and cheese, and what will barely maintain two Lowland cattle, will maintain three Highland cattle comfortably. If each of these things is taken into consideration, it is easy to ascertain that Highland cattle are the only type to take, and neither would

Highland Cattle-Beast. Photography by Sandra Edelsward.

it be difficult to transport them. Without knowing whether my
labour will come into someone's hands, who will bring about that
of which I have often dreamed, I want to attempt a guess or two
about the method I think would be best. If a person takes all the
trouble, he should also reap the rewards; that is, he should take
with him the best variety he hears about, such as the ones I used
to see at the Falkirk cattle market,[41] which came from Colonsay,
or the famous variety which the MacDonalds of Balquidder have,
or even the variety of the Stewarts in Inverscaddle, which I
presume are not bad, for I used to read in the papers that they
won prizes at the annual trials of Scotland. Three head would
suffice; that is, two year-old heifers and a year-old bull. These
would not need as much fodder as large cattle, and they would
be easier to handle at sea and after going ashore overseas. A little
hay and potatoes would suffice the whole way going over, and
once over there an hour, no harm would come to them, for every
respectable man would show kindness to a person coming on
business who was so noble as to bring a new type of cattle into

the country. A person could obtain up to four dollars for each cow that approached the bull, and I do not know whether the Gaelic Society of Montreal and Quebec might not publicly honour him for his labours. Although we are speaking about all of this, no one knows if it will ever happen; if it does, the cattle of America will be just as famous in a hundred years, as the horses are today.

Sheep.

There are not so many of the old *large sheep* in Canada that we need be long discussing them. But while there are few of them, they are very troublesome. Although the farmers do not ruin their wool by smearing them, or lose time shearing them, they must not forget them for one night, for if they do, some will never trouble them again. I saw this happen once in the Huron Tract. There was a lively, censorious gentleman who went over from Patrick's green Isle, and he saw fit to purchase a flock of sheep. The man took the flock home, and drove them into an enclosed field close to the house. Near dusk, a poor traveller, who had set out on the road, saw the sheep grazing at the edge of the field, and asked him whether he intended to take the flock in. "I do not think I will bother," he said, "there aren't any papists living within two miles of me here." This gentleman had only recently come from Ireland, and he was, as a person could tell from his speech, a firm member of the group they call *Orange-men* in that country. He thought that, once he had managed to separate himself the distance I mentioned, from the group I mentioned, no earthly enemy could offend him again. On hearing this, the traveller, who was married to a strong woman connected to the other folk, gave a slight look of reproach at the way the man answered him, and moved on. My gentleman went in and went to bed. He slept serenely, securely. He rose in the morning, and

Highland Sheep. Photography by Sandra Edelsward.

he went outside. He looked at the bare field where he had left
the flock, but when he did, what could he say when he had
nothing left to see, but one or two tattered hides, and fragments
of bones? The wolves had come at night, and they brought all
this misfortune on him, and I do not doubt that today he keeps
his sheep closer by. The emigrant will understand from this short
story how careful a man must be with sheep in Canada. They
must be put in every night, and never allowed into the forest, by
day or by night. They have the white hornless variety in Upper
Canada, and that is the most suitable type there, since their wool
is so good. And it should be good, since they sell it at a half-
dollar a pound. The wool is much more expensive than the meat;
for sheep can be purchased there, for around two dollars, at the
beginning of winter. But will that not be plenty at that time, since
they will not get a blade of grass for four or five months, except
for food from the hand? They are not susceptible to disease there.
There is no mention of mange, braxy, or diseases of the head.
Keeping them from the wild animals is the most difficult task;

but the only way to do it is to put them in at night, and not to let them far from sight by day. The new farmer who wishes to have sheep, must plant grass in due season; there is no way to keep them without green grass.

Swine.

"The worst to the last," says the proverb; and the Gaels celebrate this even better than the proverb states it. The proverb has been well used, certainly, but if it has, it has very often been at the expense of an excellent, useful animal; to wit, at the expense of the pig. Every saying is useful in its own day and time, and so this one has always been, but will it be so much longer? indeed it will not; for any man who decides not to give the pig a fighting chance as long as it lives, and the first seat at the table after its death, even on Friday, ought not to go to America, to slight the goodness of providence, disparage the pig, and offend his fellow man. The pig is the king of the animals in America; dead and alive. The pig is the first animal the new farmer must obtain, and the last animal he should part with. The pig is the first animal in which he will invest his money; yes indeed, but what is wrong with that? is it not the first one from which he will earn money, and regain his own expense threefold as well? The farmer without pigs in America, is not worth much; he is a senseless man, a useless husband, and a bad neighbour.

I will clarify this under three headings. He is a senseless man, for he is blinded by prejudice against pigs, so that his bad nature will not let him believe or admit how useful they are, and all of that, because he is so lazy that he will not work his land to provide feed for them. He is a useless husband, for he will live in poverty; his indolence will not let him raise a crop, and since he will not have a crop, he will not have bread, and since he will have no bread, he will not have a single morsel of meat either for himself, or for his family. He is a bad neighbour, for his indolence will not let him make fences to keep out his neighbour's pigs, since he has none of his own, and when they enter the poor, little crop he has, he will jump on them with stones, dogs, stakes, and guns, until even a blockhead would grasp the wretched situation. But that is only a small part of the harm he will do; he will destroy every four-footed animal that comes within a quarter mile of him; he will set a bad example for his own children and to other men's children; he will raise disputes among neighbours; he will make them anxious about their stock; he will ruin their peace and his own peace as well; he will bring pain, anguish, and toothache, sorrow, grief, and heartbreak to his wife, on account of how often he will be in conflict, brawls, and contention; and he will participate in every imaginable type of vice.

But although he who does not have pigs is a bad farmer in America, he is not a wise man who has more than he ought, for the craft of every other sort of livestock also applies to them; it is more beneficial for one to be on a diet for two, than for two to be on a diet for one. If many of them are kept on a little feed, they will not prosper; but if a man is satisfied with a number suitable for what he has to give them, they will be the most useful type of livestock a poor man can get in Canada. And neither are they difficult to obtain. A person can get a piglet, about a month or five weeks of age, for a day's work. Once they are six or seven weeks, they will support themselves in the forest, until the wintry weather stops them. And it will not stop them easily, in a year when nuts are plentiful. They will dig through the snow until they reach them among the leaves, and they will spend most of the day collecting them at a time when other animals will never think of looking for them. They collect every ear of corn left on the stubble, they make use of every apple the wind shakes from the trees, they gather every grain of seed lost around the barn, they do well finishing the scraps and peas, they eat the frozen potatoes in the winter, and the potato sprouts in the summer, and they will drink whey and buttermilk all year if they can get it. It is easy enough to feed a small, strong, little offspring of theirs, and to earn money from it, or eat it when a man cannot earn a penny any other way. And their meat will earn about a dollar and a half more than beef per hundred pounds, and if it were not worth that much, it would not get it. It seems odd to me that there is not more of a difference in the price, for every careful housewife knows that it lasts the longest, every *epicure* knows that it is the tastiest, and every educated doctor, and every sensible man who eats it knows that it is much, much healthier for dinner than beef, goat meat, or mutton. But how will the man who has never tried it have any knowledge about this matter, except for what he has learned from his father and grandfather, that is, to smile when he hears the word pork being mentioned, as if his teeth were on edge. Let that same man go to America, where he will find *pork* which has been fed properly, and dressed properly, and add a hint of hunger to sharpen his appetite, and I can assure you that the day will never come when he will say, with regard to pigs, "the worst to last."

The pigs of Canada are not usually large. I think the variety they have there is not very good, and that it would not be a bad idea to take over a *decent*, small piglet or two; sea sickness would not bother them at all, but take plenty for them to eat.

XIX

WILD ANIMALS

❧

Bears.

I have often understood, from the conversation between my countrymen and myself on America, that they have a terrible fear of the wild animals of that country. As I remarked that this stumbling block made some timid people anxious, I thought to take this opportunity to move it out of the way, or at least to erect a sign at the proper place, so that travellers will recognize it when they encounter it. And because I am approaching it, I think I will take the heavy end of it first. Is it not appropriate for me to call it the heavy end? for there is no other wild animal in Canada that has a head as heavy, and a body as strong as the black Bear. Yes, the *black* bear, for the *grizzly* bear is not in Upper Canada at all. And neither is the *black* one as numerous as some of the important Writers maintain, particularly where there is a large tract of dry land, and with hard wood growing on it. A farmer may be ten years in that type of place before he sees one of them. But he should be forewarned, that although he might not see one for ten years, it could be his livestock will see one before he has been there ten days. And if it comes after them at all, it will have something of the look of a messenger, for it will not leave empty-handed. If it goes after the pig (and it often does, for it knows its animals well), the contest will quickly go one way. It will sweep the pig up under its arm, be it big or small, and that movement will cause neither the bear nor its listeners much anxiety, for it will keep the pig from whimpering, with one kind, warm, little squeeze between the elbow and breast-bone. It performs the same trick with a sheep; but if it attacks a cow, it usually grabs it around the small of the back, tearing a strip out of its side, down to the belly, so that daylight reaches the kidneys, in a flash. It has a very noble nature; there is nothing more worthy among the four-footed. But, as I said before, a man may be ten years in Canada, without seeing or smelling one, and I knew men who were twenty years there, who never lost an animal to one, even though they raised livestock all that time. The end of autumn is the time it makes the greatest threat of destruction, and no wonder the poor animal would be very desirous of plunder at that season; for as soon as the winter storms come, it takes to its den, and thrusts its paw into its mouth, and except for sucking on that paw, neither for sporting matters nor for domestic duties, will it show its face until the earth is visible again. The black bear will not show its face to any man at any time, except for a female with cubs. If a man does not avoid a female in that situation, misfortune will be his, for if a man wounds one of the cubs, and approaches it before it is dead, he will be in more danger than it is worth. Nevertheless, if he is a lively man, swift of foot, on level ground, he might leave the mother behind, by quickly taking to his heels, for a while, but not for long on account of her powerful running pursuit of him. The black bear is almost as fast as the badger of the Highland glens, continuing to run at the same speed from dawn to dusk;

"Though it tears off in a rush,
It will not complain of its chest."

They and the Indians are at each others' throats every other week.
But if the bear happens to be asleep, the Indian will slaughter it
without its noticing until its entrails are tangled around its thighs.
If it happens that he shoots and wounds it, as soon as the bear
comes up to him, he will throw away his rifle and *tomahawk*, bow,
quiver, and every piece of equipment except for the black-dagger
alone. He always keeps the knife on his right hip, in a sheath sewn
to a kilt-girdle, which he always has tied about his waist, and he
will leave it there until he can prop his back up against a convenient tree, something not too difficult to find. As soon as the
bear reaches him, it will start with its old tricks. It will stand up
on its hind legs, and put its forelegs around him and the tree,
expecting that nothing will hinder it from squeezing the Indian's
heart out of its shell. But that will not be as easy as it had thought.
It will not be able to lay a tooth on him, and as it will not, it can
squeeze, crush, and press the tree for the rest of its life, but it
will not put a dent in the tree, and as long as the tree stands, the
Indian will be safe. Although he will be safe, that will not be
enough; he must prove himself a son worthy of his father. He
takes hold of the knife, stabbing the bear in the hip, and with
the first thrust he makes, it will let out a full-chested roar. The
music will go through the fiddle then. The entrails will be dragged
through the village, and the Indian will be on the carcass in short
order; and he will earn a good day's wage, for there is a great deal
of fat and oil on it, and both are very valuable. Its pelt is very
useful in the winter, for covering travellers who take to the road
in sleds, and it is exceedingly good as a top cover for a bed. I have
not heard of any meat that compares favourably to its meat. I
was not so fortunate as to have ever had a bear steak, but those
who know how to skin it, and eat it, used to tell me that there

was nothing like it. They led me to understand that the meat has red and white streaks in it, something like the breast stripe of a lamb, or the small of a pig's back, but much, much tastier than either of those. Although the bear is a pleasing and useful animal when it is dead, it is an ugly beast, as well as dangerous, while it is on its feet. The fur is filthy, shaggy, matted, the back is humped, and the hind legs lie on the ground, right up to the knee joint. Each of its paws is as broad as a bull's hoof, and its jaw is as wide as the opening of a peddler's sack. But although its mouth is enormous, it is, in a way, well behaved, for it rarely comes close enough to put the slightest fear into night travellers.

Wolves.

If the bear is a calm, silent animal, that is not the case with the wolf. It makes a horrific roar. When it lifts its voice, and lets out the first howl, I do not know just what I could compare it to. A twelve-pronged antlered stag, bellowing in a narrow, rocky, cavernous glen, around the dead of midnight, during the calm weather of the rutting season, is the only thing I know like it. Whether it does this to amuse itself, or to bother others, I cannot say or understand; but certainly, it inspires fear in the heart of many a poor stranger, newly arrived in the country. On a quiet night, they get into a complete frenzy; for they can hear one another so far away, that they can neither stop nor rest from answering each other until the half-light of dawn banishes them to the secrecy of the den. But if they set out for the den, it is not without having something to chew the cud, if they can. Everything is like a fish in the net for them. They are equally accomplished at taking horses, cattle, sheep, pigs, chickens, and ducks; but if they can take their pick of the animals I have mentioned, they much prefer sheep. Even if only one of them is involved in killing sheep, if it gets enough time to set things to its liking, it will not leave even a piece of the sheep's ear as witness to the deed. A teazing or two of wool is the largest thing a person should expect to see. They are much more plentiful, like every other wild animal, where the land is low and wet, and where there is a pine forest. They often go about in packs in remote places like that; and there is no escape for any living creature they meet. If there happens to be a large number of them, with the slightest hunger pang, they will not hesitate to attack even a man. The Indians often engage in physical combat with them. The most singular and famous trial, of this sort, I have heard of, happened somewhere far up the *Ottowa*. A valiant warrior of the heroic men we are talking about, went out one day to find food, or so he and the rest of his family thought; but a person scarcely knows in the morning what will happen before night falls. The brave hero was looking for a strong, swift-footed herd; but alas! the ravenous pack of wolves encircled him, with intent to put an end forever to his hunting and to his labouring. There was no one there to see or to relate how vigorously they attacked each other: and that is just as well; for even if there were fifty soldiers present, I do not know if any of them could have made it away from the field of battle; but if each man among them did as the Indian did, he would have. Did he not succeed in marking them by splitting their heads open? His people went out the next day to seek his dead body. They found nine wolves, lifeless, side by side at the foot of a large birch tree, and the *tomahawk* of the champion up to its haft in the skull of the ninth one. They knew from this that their mighty hero had put his strong back against the tree, when he noticed the danger encircling him, and, with the light, trifling tool he had in his strong grasp, he struck each one that attacked him, until the *tomahawk* was caught by accident in the head of the ninth, so that he did not get it out as quickly as he needed in order to finish the job. It can be imagined that they were not long in finishing him off once they got at him. There

Wolf Hunt, Drawn and Engraved by J. Jackson, after a Picture by Snyders, in One Hundred and Fifty Woodcuts, *1835.* Photography by Axel Menzefricke.

was not a single strand of his hair to be seen. The black-dagger he wore was at the foot of the tree, without a trace of its carrying belt; furthermore, not even its sheath. Only that, and a fragment or two of his outer clothing, were found. His rifle was found a short distance away, where he threw it down, they surmised, when he made for the foot of the tree.

But although wolves are numerous in some places, as may be understood from what I have related, they are not so numerous throughout the whole country. A farmer may go ten years without seeing or sensing a single one of them. A wolf will never approach a man, and neither will it try to kill an animal larger than a yearling. Large cattle will repel it, in spite of its attempts, as long as only one comes. And although two were to come, the cattle would not be afraid, unless it were in the spring, when they were lean.

The wolf is swift, strong; thickset at the front, and slender at the rear; it has pointed ears, which stand up straight, and a long, low, extending tail; —

"Its middle is broad, its chest is ragged;
Its joints crooked, its hough bent."

Foxes, &.

Foxes are as numerous in the forests of America as sheep are in Ben Doran, and, I dare say, even more numerous. They are the small, full-bellied, plains variety; or, as they are usually referred to, the "black-footed." Just as those ones over there are no different from these ones here in colour and in shape, so too they are alike in nature. They do not often bother the farmer, or anything that belongs to him; but he and the women will be cursing them every other day for snatching hens. Perhaps there is no other animal in the entire world so adept at this pastime as the red fox of Canada. It creeps through the corn, and the grass, until it is so close to the doorpost as to be certain of its success. It often takes a full half-dozen in a day. There is another, fleet-footed variety, called the *silver fox*; but although I encountered plenty of red foxes in Canada, I was not so fortunate as to meet the *silver fox*; and I have never seen one, small, big, or middling. I saw plenty of badgers, however, and martens, and the rest of the small pole-cat-like beasts. They are all just as they are at home, in shape and in nature. There are many other varieties of small beasts – such as woodchucks; and black, red, and dappled squirrels. These, and the badgers, make a very good broth. I knew a gentleman who went out from Edinburgh, who was accustomed to using them, and they were justly praised. He would eat the meat first, and then drink the juice; and why not? as the true proverb says –

"He who eats his sow,
May sup her broth."

There are wild rabbits in some places, and white hares, of the same variety that are found on hill tops in the Highlands. But what has happened to me, for I have forgotten

"Those of the white buttocks,
And the red mantles?"

The deer are very plentiful in many districts of Canada; but it is not the type we used to know, when we were

"Taking to the deer forest,
And ascending the rugged country;"

but rather a type with long, slender tails down to the hough. The underside of the tail is completely white; and, usually,

When they rush off,
Through the trees of the great forest,

they swing the tail over the ridge of their backs, like a young foal after feeding, going out for the first time in the spring. A person will see only the odd little glimpse of them between the trees, when they get under way; and, because their hindquarters are so white, a stranger might think they are completely white. But this is not so.

"Their aspect is coloured a soft yellow,
They are red in form and appearance,"

and a man may hunt them without reserve. The bailiff, "constable, if not hound," is not so hard-hearted as to say that it is wrong. Certainly, they suffer hardship in the winter; but even so, they forget it completely in the summer.

"They will have rolls of fat
Covering their rumps;
And their bare, handsome, and proud breasts."

There is a type of red hen in Canada that is somewhat akin to our own partridge in colour, but is about the size of the moor hen. These are very good to eat. They have no flaws, except that there are so few of them.

There are kites, eagles, hawks, and owls.

There are countless numbers of wood pigeons. These are much more damaging to crops, and bothersome to the country folk of Canada, than the rooks are to those on the Lowland plains.

The snakes are as plentiful in Upper Canada as midges are in the Black Forest of Rannoch on a July night, and much more plentiful; but they are completely harmless.

Passenger-Pigeon, Drawn and Engraved by Messrs. Sly and Wilson, from a Print in Wilson's "American Ornithology," in One Hundred and Fifty Woodcuts, *1835.* Photography by Axel Menzefricke.

XX

FLIES, &C.

❧

Of all the kinds of creatures that vex the emigrant when he reaches the new country, none is half as troublesome to him as the Indian fly, or, as the English call it, the *musquitoe*. Like every other nasty beast, it is fond of taking hold of the stranger; and it has a bloody grip. As soon as summer is well begun, it awakens, and begins to flutter about. It gives off a hissing hum, something like the droning of wasps, and, without any delay, it begins its mischief. It is about the size of the black, flying ant, which is found throughout the Highland forests, with a long proboscis. And if the proboscis is long, it is correspondingly hard; for it is as expert at boring into a person through his clothing, as it would be if he were bare. A person who has recently arrived in the country will find that his skin often rises in blisters, after they have bitten him, just as if he had been scourged with a thicket of nettles; and, indeed, some people always break out like that. The Indian fly is like all other bad goods here, five hundred times more abundant where the land is wet, foul, and low-lying, and in the forest of pine and cedar, than it is where the land is dry and high, with sparse hardwood growing on it. Although it does not often get the opportunity to kill men completely, I do know of one or two instances when it took people's lives; and even if a person were as strong as a giant, he could not battle long against the flies in America in the summer, unless he were close to a bonfire, or out of the forest, where the sun could shine on him. But in spite of the harm they cause, they cannot do the slightest bit of damage to any person, except in the shade. Some use a tobacco pipe to keep them away; and they succeed with that, as long as they keep it in their mouths, blowing smoke about their ears: but as soon as they let up, undoubtedly they will regret it. The fly has a very keen nose, and it will locate smokers by the bad smell of their breath, so that they are often worse off. But even though they are troublesome in the day, at night they are worse, by far. Once they get into the houses, a person will get neither rest by day, nor sleep at night, with them. There is no way at all of getting the upper hand on them over there, except with sulphur smoke.

The Woodcutters (Dunn Township near Port Maitland, Ontario), c. 1840, Sarah Ann Carter. Courtesy of the Metropolitan Toronto Reference Library. T14800.

There is another exceedingly large gadfly in Canada, which is four times the size of the green cleg of Scotland. This one does not arrive so early, and neither does it stay as long as the smaller one. It is five hundred times less common than the *musquitoe*, and neither should it be as common; for if it were, there would be no king nor lord in America other than itself.

There is another variety of fly, enough to put fear into the stranger at night, even though he will never see it in the daytime. This is the kind they call the firefly. It is seen darting back and forth all night, like bolts of lightning. But in this instance, the arrival of the first frost will put a sudden end to its beauty, and to the evils of the rest, all at once.

Conclusion

When a person is about to write a book, he must give it a beginning; and just as certainly, he must give it an ending. The large book has a beginning and an end; that is the whole of it, and although my little book is small, it can not appear without both of these. First I gave it a beginning, and I leave it up to the Reader to determine whether I have done that part of my work correctly. I am now going to conclude it, while knowing full well that many of my readers will say that I have done what is necessary, but in an exceedingly imperfect, careless, and defective manner. But it is not from a feeling of guilt, or from a sense of not fulfilling my duty, that I say this at all. I actually think every emigrant to whom my work comes will assume the book was made for his own personal needs, (and in a sense it is so), and that he will say, when he has read it up to this point: – "Useless Guide! he did not think of guiding me the way I wished to go. He scarcely mentioned *Cape Breton*, where my dear brothers are; or *Nova Scotia*, where my two beloved sisters are; or *New Brunswick*, where my good uncle is. No, no; only Canada. Canada, Canada; nothing but Canada." As I would like to escape from the harsh reproof of this dear man, I think that it will be proper for me to explain to him the importance of the occupation of a guide, and how hard the rules are, by which he is judged. The occupation of guide, is a very important occupation; people's lives and wealth both depend on him. The law is very hard on a guide; if he undertakes to bring a ship into a port that he does not know, and it ends up on a skerry through his error, he will be punished and given a dreadful bruising; he will lose his reputation and credibility, and every man he places in danger, and every person who hears a report of his deed, will curse him. But the guide who knows a harbour will be bad, that it will have a bad bottom, that

Corduroy Road Over a Swamp in Orillia Township, Ontario, September 1844,
Titus Hubbert Ware. Courtesy of the Metropolitan Toronto Reference Library.
T14377.

there will be a lack of shelter, and that every ship entering it will be in danger every moment until it gets out; but, who, nevertheless, offers to guide it and set it ashore, he will not be shown any kindness, mercy, or respect, except by having his head severed from his body immediately. What will my gentleman say to this? I certainly would not guide him to a place I had never been! far from it; and how much less would I guide him to a region about which I had heard many bad reports, toiling, rather, with him a little further to a country which I and other men know to be a good place. It is a terribly foolish matter for a person, if he wishes to emigrate at all, not to go to the best place, if he can. The passage to *Quebec* is only about a crown more per person, than it is to the *Cape*, or to the other regions we mentioned; and as for saying that Canada is a better country, I do not think that we need bother with that, for all intelligent men are unanimous on that point already. Neither do they differ in their opinions on the *Cape*; there is no doubt at all that it is not the choicest settlement in America. It is small wonder, as many things make it worse than other places. We have neither space nor time to name all of them here; but, nonetheless, we will point out one or two things in passing: – It is the coldest and has the worst land, and because of this, those who have money and are well informed are setting out for Canada, and leaving the *Cape* behind them. It is also the closest and the least expensive to reach, and because it is, many *poor* Gaels went there first, and because they went, many of their poor relatives will follow them. The *poorest* folk who live in America came from Scotland; the *poorest* folk in America live there, and the *poorest* folk who go to America from Scotland continue to go there, and when all the *poor* are sent there, I believe they will be enough to make poverty.[42] It may be understood from this short account that we completely refuse to guide pilgrims to the *Cape*. It is not that we are seeking to keep the Gaels out if they wish to go there, but we would like to ask of those, whom we encounter as we set

sail, what is taking them there. It might be that they have relatives there, and, because they do, they wish to join them. They
will expect to obtain lodgings for a week, or perhaps for a month,
until they can find something for themselves, and even if they
do not happen to obtain that as quickly as they would like, they
will think no harm can come to them, as long as they are with
their friends and relatives. That is all very well, but my advice to
the head of the house is to make an effort to go to the best
country, to the country with the wealthiest men, and to the
country where it is easy for himself and his family to have something for themselves, that no one can take away from them. Any
man contemplating going to America, because a relative went
before him, should heed this warning from me, and he should
stay at home. Who showed kindness to his kinsman when he went
over before him? did he not survive by his own perseverance? other
men must do likewise. He had no opportunities when he arrived,
that men do not have today, and men may now have even one or
two more. Let them labour as he did, and they will have as much
as he; but if they do not, is it reasonable that he should maintain them? And even if it were reasonable, a change occurs in the
mind of a man, after he goes to America, that the Gaels do not
understand. A lazy man is rare in America, and because he is, they
do not like to be bothered by lazy people. The man who starts
out poor, is encouraged by how well he gets on, and he strives
with all his heart to reach the same standard as the man who
started out with some means. The man who starts out with some
means, on the other hand, is annoyed and galled because the man
who began at a disadvantage is catching up to him, and thus he
is so fierce and so stubborn in every situation, that he will not
allow even a cat to get in his way. The emigrant may understand
from this, that, if he goes to his kinsman, he will have to work
for him, and if he does not expect to do this, he will not grow
much older before he understands the truth of the proverb, which

Lands in Upper Canada, to be disposed of by The Canada Company, Canada Company, 1832. Courtesy of the J.J. Talman Regional Collection, The D.B. Weldon Library, The University of Western Ontario, London. C921.

says: — "friendship is as it is kept." Let the emigrant, who has family, take *counsel* from the "guide," and let him place his trust in the goodness of providence, which bestows on him health and the ability to earn a living in a good country, through his own diligence; and not

"Entrust the matter to his brother,
Though he were his own mother's son,"

once he goes ashore on the western side of the Atlantic.

The things which we pointed out about the *Cape* may be applied, to a certain extent, to *Nova Scotia, New Brunswick,* &c. The head of the family should avoid them, but make his way as directly as he can to *Canada.* But as for the man who is not interested in land or a settled home for himself and his offspring, but only in day labour, he may find enough work in the *Cape,* &c. They transport a great deal of timber out of these regions, and there is a need for lads to cut it and place it on board ships. They mine coal there, and do many other dirty jobs of that nature, which a person who goes to *Upper Canada* need not expect. There will be a little money coming in, for the man who works at these jobs, at the end of the month or the week, but even if that is so, there are also many things that will take it away again.

Any man who works in the ports, and in the towns, is liable to many expenses that do not trouble the person in the country from one end of the year to the other. He will have many companions — some of them are good, and some do as they please. They will be boarded at the inn; they will look forward to a party every night they get their weekly-wage; and they will be considered mean-spirited if they do not conduct their affairs in this fashion, right from the beginning. They will be treated very kindly as long as these diversions continue; but,

When a dollar forsakes them,
And their purses are plundered,

they will be shown another treatment. As a certain kinsman among the best Gaelic bards said —

"While there is milk in your breasts,
You will be tranquilly and steadily sucked,
Until your bosom is dry, and
Then, you will be thrown out on the street."

I am now going to bid farewell to the "Emigrant," and wish him success and a good journey. I would like to believe that he will make good use of my work; nevertheless, these words of the poet come to me: —

"For the young man without wealth,
    It is a useless affair to seek respect;
Though he speak with understanding,
    It is one in a hundred who will listen to him."

THE END.

Appendix I

Diary of Robert MacDougall, 1 Jan. - 14 Feb. 1842, on a voyage from England to Port Phillip, Australia on the ship *Manlius*.[43] Robert MacDougall ultimately made Australia his home.

Jan 1 – A strong breeze of quarter wind, and weather somewhat cold – Three vessels in sight. This being New Years day, the Captain is *kind* enough to treat all on Board to a glass of whisky – a favour which is appreciated by none, on board, less than by the unworthy writer of these notes, as he apprehends another attack of fever soon, and can hardly be convinced that *even grog* can be proof against it, from the symtoms he display's – his tongue being foul and parched – his head dissy – his eye sight dim: – in short his whole frame, and system, thoroughly deranged.

The foregoing part of these notes is carefully abstracted from a form of a Journal kept by one Mr James Smith, who was a passenger on board; and pointedly compased with my own experience during the remainder of the voyage – a period which I passed in great anxiety of mind and affliction of body, owing to my being confined with the foul and fatal disorder; which, about this time, prevailed almost universally on Board.

2 - Perfectly calm in the morning – Started a fresh breeze about noon. A number of the Passengers very ill; particularly Mrs Robertson, from Baideanach and P--- Madigan and family convalescent.

3 - A gentle breeze of fair winds – One sail in sight – Fever raging furiously and assuming a more fatal aspect daily.

4 - A Strong breeze of fair wind – Ship going at the rate of 10 knots. Sickness increasing. I spent the two preceding days in a most miserable state: the swet running in torrents of my head; nevertheless the lower extremeties of my body almost stuff with cold – Mrs Robertson also very ill.

5 - Wind still fair – One sail in sight. Sickness very prevalent on board.

6 - A strong breeze of fair wind and our ship going at a gallant rate. Sickness assuming an alarming aspect – Mrs Robertson and me among the worse cases.

7 - A fair wind still and Studing sails set. A great many bad cases of sickness on board.

8 - A constant breeze of foul wind which rendered it nescessary to steer N.E. Sickness still increasing in all the different apartments in the Ship.

The Gallon Measure, with which the water was given out, suspected to be deficient by the Passengers, and according, brought to the test; where, and when, it is satisfactorily proven to be five Scotish Gills a wanting – Captain threatened, and that deservedly, for using the same, by both cabin and Steerage

Passengers.

9 - Wind right a head but moderate. The fever raging with unabated fury —
Mrs Robertson and me blistered and under the same treatment.

10 - Calm with heavy rain in the fornoon. Sickness still increasing — A man
named Henry dead.

11 - A fresh breeze — Ship going from 8 to 9 knots an hour. Another man dead
this afternoon. A sail in sight about Sunset.

12 - Blowing fresh with showers of rain — Ship going about 8 knots.

13 - Rainy and rather disagreeable — Sickness increasing Mrs Robertson despaired
of, and some others very ill.

14 - Blowing somewhat fresh with showers occasionaly. Sickness prevailing to
a great extent. Mr. Ewart, a married Gentleman from Belfast, (who, along with
his family, proved very kind and of great service to me hither to) complain-
ing, and apparently under the influence of the cursed and foul disorder.

15 - Still blowing fresh — A sea foul [fowl], caught, which measured 10 feet
between the two extremeties of the wings.

16 - Wind foul but moderate. A good many of the Passengers dangerously ill
— Mr. Ewart, who lay in the Berth next to me, very feverish.

17 - Wind still ahead. Mrs Ross from Edinburgh very ill, as also Mrs Robertson.

18 - A perfect calm — Some of the officers of, in one of the Boats, Shooting
sea foul [fowl]. Mr. Ewart, Mrs Ross and Mrs Robertson very ill — A child
dead and hove overboard soon after.

A good breeze of fair wind in the afternoon.

19 - A gentle breeze of kind wind. Mrs Robertson and another child dead.

20 - A sail in sight — proved to be the Palastine of London, bound for Sydney
with Passengers: all well. Certainly very fortunate when compaired with us, miserable beings, dying daily; and no prospect, at present, of the sickness abating.
Mrs Ross dead about noon

21 - A gentle breeze — Sea very smooth. Mr. Ewart & me very ill.

22 - Wind still fair and Studing sails set — About 50 Sick on board and and an
elderly woman named Mrs Murphey speechless.

23 - Fair and pleasant with Stunsail set. A number of the sick very ill — Mrs
Murphey and another child dead.

24 - Wind increasing and still fair. Ship running about 9 knots an hour. Mr.
Ewart, and his humble Servant, getting easier, and beginning to comfort each
other by relating our sensations severally.

25 - A fair wind — Ship going at the rate of 10 knots — The Island St. Paul in
sight. A child dead on board.

26 - Wind still fair - a man named Donald MacKinnon from Sky very ill —
Another child dead.

27 - A fresh breeze — Ship going about 9 knots — I feel a little better today, as
also does my esteemed friend Mr. Ewart.

28 - Wind fair and Strong and our Craft going about 8 knots. A number of the sick folks recovering; but others dangerously ill.

29 - Ship going about 6 knots an hour on her proper course. Mr. Ewart & myself getting better and, behold! commencing to sup sowance.

30 - Wind still continueing to be fair. About a dozen of Dr. Smart's patient getting better.

31 - A fine breeze of fair wind and Ship going at the rate of 7 knots. I plucked up, and, with the assistance of a young man, named Henry Baxter, came out of bed, but could not, as yet, stand on my feet – Mr Ewart still improving.

Feb. 1 - Weather most beautiful – Studing sails set and sip going 7 knots. Came out of bed and a basinfull of sowance from my Benefactress, Mrs Ewart. Mr Mawhood re-attacked with the fever.

2 - Weather delightful – Got on deck for the first time, after my illness, Mr Ewart out of bed, and sitting in front of his Berth. D. McKinnon a good deal Better.

3 - Most beautiful weather. About 10 ten of the Sick, who are recovering on deck - a number of fresh patients lying down.

4 - Calm weather – a great many of the sick on deck. Doctor rejoicing for his success in restoring their health.

5 - A strong breeze of Tuad wind. A boy, about 4 years of age, belonging to Mr. Scot, the Englishman, inopt through the nescessary part and was drowned instantaneously - the Ship being under such away that it was an impossibility to save him.

6 - Wind a head – Two deaths on Board.

7 - Perfectly calm in the forenoon – Shooting carried on, by the Doctor, Mate, &c., extensively and some foul [fowl] killed. A fine breeze in the afternoon.

8 - A stuff breeze from the N. – Ship going 9 knots on an average. Sickness prevailing to a great extent. An old woman and a child dead.

9 - Strong wind and rain occasionally. A few more lying ill – Mawhood very ill, and declared by all, except the Surgeon, to be *"A Gone Succour."*

10 - A fair breeze and Ship going about 9 knots. Anchors, chains, &c., cleared out, and other preparations made for our arrival. A man dead.

11 - A gentle breeze of s.w. wind. Mrs Stewart, the Socialist's wife, who has been ill for some time, dead and another young man.

12 - A moderate breeze. No deaths.

13 - Most beautiful weather – The Australian coast descerned from the Main-top, about 4 P.M.

14 - A fair breeze – the main land on our larboard bow - all on the alert except those who are lying ill below. Among this number lyeth the unfortunate Mawhood, staring like a Racoon in the month of March, longing for a blade of green grass to refresh his inactive jaws

Came to Anchor, in the far-famed Portphillip about 5 in the afternoon

Appendix II

Letter by Robert MacDougall in *The Victorian Agricultural and Horticultural Gazette* 1.1 (21 March 1857): 5-6,44 published in Melbourne, Australia.

Regarding Livestock

The following interesting letter was addressed to the "Argus," which we republish for the benefit of our country readers: —

SIR, - You are often reminding us, your Agricultural readers, how far behind hand we are in the Colony in the march of improvement. We receive your hints, too, I think I may safely say, in a proper spirit; yet it strikes us rather forcibly that our brother-Colonists who follow "pastoral pursuits," require a "word in season" just as much as we do. To give your readers generally an idea that the Squatters of this country are not by any means "up to the mark" in their own simple and primitive calling, perhaps you will be good enough to give this extract an insertion in the world-read "Argus: -

"SHEEP. — The 'Yorkshire Gazette,' of the 1st instant, states that at Market Weighton, on Wednesday last, Mr. Thomas Mitchell exhibited the celebrated three-year-old Cotswold ram "Champion," bred by Thomas B. Browne, Esq., Hampen, Gloucestershire, which has taken prizes at all the leading Agricultural shows in England, Ireland, and Paris, and considered by all judges to be the most wonderful animal of the sheep kind ever seen in Yorkshire. His estimated weight is about 100 lbs. per quarter."

The Cotswold sheep, Sir, for anything I know, have been only introduced in *one* instance yet into Victoria, namely by that determined friend of progress, William Lyall, Esq., of Western Port. And yet it can be satisfactorily shown that this sheep is capable of being brought into the Melbourne market from the plains of Victoria, prime mutton, at the age of two years, or *under*, weighing 120 lbs. At the same time, this animal yields a moderately valuable and an immensely heavy fleece, and could be advantageously reared on lands here that can never be profitably occupied with the breed of sheep we cultivate at present in the country. To enable us, indeed, to avail ourselves of all the pastorage of Victoria, with due regard to profit and economy, there is still another breed of sheep that must be introduced, the Chevoit [sic]. Upon some other occasion I may take the liberty of shewing you, Sir, how our exports, as well as the meat for the million, would be prodigiously increased by the introduction of the two varieties of sheep I have now mentioned.

While saying something upon this subject, I may also mention, that with

regard to the cattle of the Colony we are almost equally far behind. We have
never yet introduced the breed that would enable us to procure an ample
supply of prime fat cattle at an early age, too from those high, cold, coarsely
grassed districts that at present glut our market with store cattle, at the
average age of seven years old. We have certainly imported the short-horns
in small numbers, and also the Herefords. The former will occupy our richest
districts more profitably than any other variety of cattle; and the latter are
remarkably well adapted for runs a shade colder and coarser and farther from
market than those that are really suitable for short-horns.

But our selections are still incomplete. We must forthwith have the "Black
Doddie" from the "Land-of-cakes." This is the Ox to "keep this courage
cherrie" on the hill side. Nature adapted him beyond any other for the wilds
of Australia. Farmer-like speaking, he is thoroughly and efficiently thatched.
He supports himself on poor fare — arrives early at maturity — travels with
ease and without waste to market, and is allowed by the greatest authority
in the world (the Emperor of France) to be the finest beef in the universe.
If our motto be PROGRESS, Sir, we must have this breed, without a year's
delay, and in its purity too, from the fountain head, the immortal William
McCombie. This gentleman, who, I am happy to say, is brother to our fellow-
Colonist, the Hon. Thomas McCombie, has done, in perfecting the black-
polled cattle of Scotland, as much as Bakewell and Colling did in their day
to their own favourite breeds in England. In short, he has succeeded so mar-
vellously in adjusting their symmetrical proportions that they are now the
admiration not only of the natives of their own far north, but of the breeders of England, Ireland, France, and the Continent of Europe. Not to digress
farther, the man who shall bring them here shall not lose his reward, I feel
confident. Mr. Lyall, I am creditably informed, gets £ 100 for the services of
his Cotswold ram to fifty ewes; and my own prize bull, Lord Nelson, (No.
13,208 in Coate's Herd Book) earned for me this season, £ 100 for services to
ten cows sent to him, over and above attending sedulously to the affairs of
a family of fifty cows at home. I merely mention this, Sir, to encourage some
gentleman who has means and opportunity, to import the second most valuable cattle now known in the world to Victoria. We only want for the sham-
bles, shorthorns, Hereford's and Black Doddies; and for the dairy we ought
to be now breeding the best of Ayrshires. No other breed except the four
above enumerated ought to be tolerated in this country.

I am, Sir, &c.,

ROBERT MCDOUGAL, Glenroy.

Appendix III

The obituary of Robert MacDougall, taken from *The Age*, Melbourne 29 June 1887.[45]

The Late Mr. Robert McDougall

The remains of the late Mr. Robert McDougall, who died at Ellora, Moonee Ponds, on Saturday last, were buried yesterday in the Melbourne General Cemetery. The funeral service was read by the Rev. H. McKail, of Bulla, the deceased being interred in the Presbyterian division, immediately in the rear of the grave of the late James McPherson Grant. Amongst those who attended the funeral were nearly all the members of the council of the National Agricultural Society of Victoria, of which body the late Mr. McDougall was a few years since an active member. Many residents of the Keilor district, where Mr. McDougall had lived for some 15 years past, also took part in the last rites. The pall bearers were all relatives of the deceased, amongst them being his only son, Mr. A. McDougall; his father-in-law, Mr. E. Rankin, of Ascotvale; and his sons-in-law, Messrs. A. Cameron and A. Smith. The late Mr. McDougall was born on the 16th April, 1813, on a cold sheep farm at the foot of Shiechallion, in the parish of Fortingall, Perthshire. The first 17 years of his life were spent on the farm, and then he removed to the western isles of Inverness and Ross, where he remained for six years. At that time the immense fishing capabilities of the seas in which these isles are situated were unknown, save to a few sportsmen. Here Mr. McDougall, who was an enthusiastic fisherman, spent his time pleasantly enough fishing and otter hunting. In 1830 he sailed for Canada, and for three years lived on the Huron Track [sic], then a new settlement. He did not take to Canadian life, and returned again to his native land. Finding that many of his acquaintances had, during his absence, departed for Australia, he decided to follow their example, and emigrate. After a 16 weeks' voyage, he landed in Port Phillip in November, 1841. He found the pastoral interest in a very depressed condition, owing to the sudden and great depreciation in the value of both live stock and wool. Soon after landing Mr. McDougall undertook the management of the herd of cattle kept by Messrs. T. and S. Learmonth, at Ercildoune. Like most Highlanders he was an expert manager of cattle, and in 1848 he commenced cattle-breeding on his own account, renting a portion of the Glenroy estate from the late D. Kennedy, and his first stock were a dozen well-bred heifers, which he bought from Messrs. Gardiner and Fletcher, of Mooroolbark. The prosperity consequent upon the discovery of gold in

Victoria gave him the opportunity he had looked for, and in 1853 he went to Tasmania, and bought the two Auroras, mother and daughter, from the late Mr. Theodore Bartley, of Launceston, whose stock were from the Van Diemen's Land Company's stud. In 1855 he again went to Tasmania, and bought from the Van Diemen's Land Company eight very fine cows, and from these are descended the finest animals in the Arundel herd. From Cona Mr. McDougall removed to a property near Essendon, which he rented from the late Mr. Aitken, who came to the colonies in the same vessel as Mr. McDougall. Another fellow-passenger was the late Mr. David McLaws, of Tower-hill, near Koroit, and it is a notable thing that several of the passengers by this ship, who came to Australia equipped with little more than stout hearts and willing hands, all became successful colonists, and died wealthy. About 16 years ago Mr. McDougall purchased the Arundel estate from the late Mr. Edward Wilson, and he resided there till a few days before his death. The story of his life from 1853 is a record of the stud herd he founded; a herd that is favourably known to cattle-breeders throughout the wide bounds of Australia. When the prospect looked darkest for the owners of cattle, Mr. McDougall never relaxed in his efforts to improve his herd by the importation of the best blood he could secure in the old country. In 1859, Mr. McDougall visited England, and purchased some stud bulls, but in this, as well as several other shipments, he had more or less misfortune through high-priced animals dying on the passage to the colonies. He was in England a second time in 1870, when he bought from Mr. T. C. Booth, of Warlaby, the white bull Field Marshal Booth, than a calf, and Major Booth, both of which sires proved of immense value in the Arundel herd. His last importation was in 1883, when he brought out the Farewell bull Sir Roderick, which soon after arrival took champion prize at the National Agricultural Society's show in Melbourne. Mr. McDougall was a thoroughly skilled stock breeder, and had made a careful study of the subject for the greater portion of his life. He had great knowledge and experience, and on all matters relating to cattle breeding he held strong opinions, which in public controversy he was apt to urge with more force of language than those opposed to him liked. For over 40 years of his life his best efforts were given to improve the breed of cattle in his adopted country, and owing to his energy, skill, and great judgment he achieved a great success. For a short time Mr. McDougall sat in the Victorian Parliament, but politics were not to his taste, and it is as a breeder of stud shorthorns that for many a year to come the name of Robert McDougall will be familiar "as a household word" with the breeders of high-class cattle in Australia. For many months past Mr. McDougall has been in failing health. He was in his 75th year, and leaves a widow and six children, one son and five daughters, to mourn their loss.

The Life of Robert MacDougall:

Biographical Information

April 16, 1813

Born in Fortingall Parish, Perthshire, Scotland, son of Alexander MacDougall, a shepherd or grazier of Foss, and wife Girsel Stewart of the ancient family of Garth Stewarts. Rob was the youngest of eight children: Peter, born 1799, married cousin Margaret Stewart c. 1831, emigrated to Canada 1833; William, born 1801; Alexander, born 1802; John (married), born 1805, emigrated to Canada 1833; Donald, born 1807; Archibald, born 1809; Anne, born 1811; Robert, born 1813. After Girsel's death in 1814 (aged 36 years), Alexander married Christian Menzies and had two more children, Hugh, born 1820 and Katherine, born 1821; Katherine, or "Miss Kitty," went to Canada with Robert and father Alexander in 1836.

c. 1830

Moved to the Hebrides, possibly following those of his brothers who were employed by their Stewart uncles. Peter MacDougall worked for his uncle, Donald Stewart, Factor of Harris (and married his daughter Margaret); and there was another uncle, Archibald Stewart, tacksman at Scuderburgh, Skye. Rob's obituary says he spent his time fishing and otter hunting (*Age*), but more probably he, like Peter, was working for one of the Stewarts.

1836-1839

Came to Canada in 1836 with his sister Kitty and father Alexander to join brothers Peter and John. Peter and John bought land in the recently-surveyed Goderich Township (Huron Tract, owned by the Canada Company) in 1833. The family story says

Peter was a cattleman who brought Highland cattle with him from Scotland; unfortunately, they died during the first winter, when he was unable to provide enough feed for them — evidently the Canada Company advertising had led him to expect "luxuriant pasture twelve months of the year" (*Goderich Township Families* 197). Peter MacDougall complained to the Canada Company about its false advertising — to no avail, of course. This may have inspired Rob's emphasis in the *Guide* on the importance of grass as a crop, as well as his denunciation of misleading reports about Canada.

It is not entirely clear why Robert came to Canada; quite often family members followed relatives who had already emigrated. But family tradition has it that Rob was somehow connected with the Canada Company and intended, right from the start, to write a book about the Company's Huron Tract settlement (see *Goderich Township Families* and Thompson family papers). It was also the contention of Peter and Margaret's grand-daughter Clarissa Elliott Thompson that, through his Canada Company connections, Rob secured a post office in the MacDougall home, with Mrs. MacDougall as postmistress (*Goderich Township Families* 198), so that he could send regular reports back to the Company's headquarters in England.

Nor is it clear why Rob returned to Scotland; nonetheless, by 1840 he was back in his homeland.

c. 1839-1841
Worked in the offices of Norman MacLeod's Gaelic periodical, *Cuairtear nan Gleann* (*Typographia* 211).

1840
Published *Tam o'Shanter*, a Gaelic translation of Robert Burns' poem, plus some of his own poetry.

1841

Published *The Emigrant's Guide to North America*.

November 1841

Departed for Australia on the *Manlius*. The decision to go seems to have been sudden. It could be that many of his friends had moved there (Ellis 72), and he decided to join them. Or perhaps he was encouraged to write a Gaelic emigration book on Australia. Because of his work with Norman MacLeod, he met Thomas Rolph, a land agent for the Canadian government, author of many books urging people to move to Canada, and writer of one book urging people to stay away from Australia. If this were the case, and Rolph had some influence in the decision, Rob would have been expecting to write something rather disparaging about Australia. A third option comes from the family history; MacDougall legends say that it was Rob's intention to return to Canada after publishing his book:

> However, after giving his report [on Canada] at a banquet in Glasgow, he was approached by a sea captain who asked him how soon he could be ready to go to Australia to prepare a similar report. "Eight o'clock tomorrow morning" was the prompt answer, to which the Captain replied: "Very well; I was about to sail at midnight, but I can hold my ship until then." (Thompson family papers)

This sounds like the Rob MacDougall of *The Emigrant's Guide*.

The *Manlius* became a plague ship; many passengers died. Rob's diary graphically chronicles the problems encountered on the voyage.

February 1842

Arrived in Port Phillip; the ship was quarantined for twelve weeks.

1842

Became herdmaster for Thomas Learmonth at Ercildoune.

1848

Rented land on the Glenroy estate; bought stock, began raising and breeding Shorthorn cattle, and built up a herd. Rob called his farm "Cona" after a Scottish glen near Fort William and Ben Nevis (Ellis 72).

1853

Married Margaret Rankin (1834-1913) of Hobart, Tasmania. They raised one son and five daughters: Caroline, born 1854; Jane, born 1856 (?); Alexander, born 1858; Margaret, born 1860; Grace, born 1862; Ann Helena, born 1872.

November 1856

Elected to the Legislative Assembly for West Bourke.

August 1857

Retired from the Assembly with "ironical memories" of his experiences there (Ellis 74).

1858

Edited a herd book on cattle for the colony. He had some difficulty getting other breeders to co-operate; because of his strong beliefs and his tendency to be outspoken, Rob had made some enemies among cattle breeders, as for example, Niel Black, his chief rival at fairs and exhibitions. At any rate, he published the *Australian Herd Book*, Part 1 (1858) in Melbourne.

1859

Went to England to buy stud bulls; his wife Margaret and daughter Caroline went with him. This first attempt to import

English stock was unsuccessful – his purchase died on route.

1868
   Purchased Arundel farm at Keilor.

1870
   Returned to England, again to buy stock, this time taking his wife Margaret and five of their children with him. He met his sister-in-law, Margaret (Stewart) MacDougall (Peter's widow) and his half-sister Kitty in Scotland. Margaret had returned home for a visit. After being disowned by her father years before for marrying Peter, she was given a triumphant welcome by remaining friends and family. Rob's trip was more profitable than the previous one, for he bought two prize Shorthorn Booth bulls which became famous in Australian breeding circles.

1872
   Moved to Arundel farm at Keilor.

1876
   Exposed rival breeder Niel Black's bull, Montebello, as a fraud. He had seen the real Montebello years before and remembered him perfectly. Rob was a formidable enemy:

   . . . *in cattle lore he was supreme. If Methuselah had been a Booth bull, Robert McDougall would have known all his sons and their wives and offspring, and held them in his memory with all their individual characteristics.* (Ellis 74)

Nor did his denunciation of Montebello endear him to Niel Black.

June 1887

Died, Arundel, Keilor. His estate was dispersed.

In Retrospect

Robert MacDougall was one of those rare, larger-than-life figures who make a strong impression on the people around them. Like many strong-willed, intelligent, and slightly eccentric people, he embodied a host of contradictions. He was a good friend and a formidable enemy; quick to anger and equally ready to tell a joke, even on himself; a writer of technical prose (in his *Australian Herd Book*) and a writer of poetry: "He could, too, when he liked string a rhyme with the best of them" (Ellis 74). More than one hundred years after his death, stories are still being told about the man and his work, stories passed down through his brother Peter's family in Canada. Some people live ordinary lives – others achieve the status of legend. Most certainly, Robert MacDougall comes close to the latter.

Notes

1 The original size of MacDougall's book was 5 3/4 inches by 3 3/4 inches - "portable" indeed! (Editor's note)

2 "Stuth" is a particular kind of woollen cloth (see MacLeod's dictionary).

3 "Camlet" is also a kind of hard, worsted cloth.

4 MacDougall seems to be saying that just as a fisherman is doomed to disappointment if the hooked fish (or "that which put the roe into the loch") convinces him to let it go, so too the hapless hunter will be disappointed if false expectations and misleading advertising lead him to Canada.

5 MacDougall's extended metaphor sets himself up as the shepherd, the prospective emigrants as his flock of sheep.

6 The literal translation of "sgrath" is "turf" or "sod."

7 I forgot about the jack-plane; the emigrant must have this to make axe handles. (MacDougall's note)

8 Nova Scotia. (MacDougall's note)

9 Wolfe's body was taken back to England.

10 Many of the people of "the glens" call this tool a lamhag, but I would think that the Gaelic of the Indians is better. (MacDougall's note)

11 MacDougall is struck by the similarities between the pronunciation of the Gaelic "tuagh-bheag" or "little hatchet," and the Indian word "tomahawk." Here and elsewhere he provides both words to show a link between the two languages.

12 The Gaelic "mu chasan," which means "about the feet," sounds like the Indian word "mocassin."

13 It is not clear which species of tree MacDougall means by "hollow-tree."

14 A cuddy is a young coal-fish.

15 See Smith's "Sean Dana," page 175. (MacDougall's note)

16 To MacDougall, "papoose" sounds like "patha-bus" or "thirsty-mouth."

17 MacDougall says that the Native word "Tecumseh" sounds like the Gaelic "deadh-chuimse," meaning "good-aim."

18 Sasannach. (MacDougall's note) MacDougall comments on the similarity between the Native word "Saganash" (white man) and Gaelic word "Sasannach" (Englishman). (Editor's note).

19 Another word-play is used here; the Gaelic "monadh," or "mountain," is italicized by MacDougall to remind us that "Montreal" is derived from "Mont Royale."

20 The word-play is continued with the use of italics on the Gaelic "tri," or three, for Mont-"tri"-al.

21 The Gaellic "ath-a-tuath" means "the north ford;" again, a Gaelic word resembles a Native word. Note also MacDougall's spelling of Ottawa.

22 To MacDougall, the pronunciation of Montreal resembles the Gaelic

"monadh thri allt" or "mount of three streams." Preceding word play on "tri" draws on this as well.

23 MacDougall thinks that "Rideau" sounds like the Gaelic "ruith-dubh" or "black river."

24 These are likely Durham boats.

25 Chatham township is actually on the right-hand side as one enters Upper Canada by this route — evidence of haste on MacDougall's part when writing his book.

26 This should be Grenville County; Greenville is a township beside Chatham, but MacDougall obviously means the country near Kingston in Upper Canada.

27 MacDougall is punning on Toronto; the Gaelic "tòr" means "tower," "fortification," or "castle."

28 Obviously McDougall did not like the cold.

29 MacDougall uses the Gaelic "abhainn na gàirich" or "roaring river" because of its similarity in sound to "Niagara."

30 Canada Company. (MacDougall's note)

31 MacDougall seems to be saying that the emigrants do not have the money to pay for their land, but gladly accept the bill.

32 MacDougall does not have a word for "maple tree" or for "sugar maple;" throughout his book, he uses "sugar-tree."

33 This is the Maitland River.

34 Crown Land.

35 Assisted emigration.

36 These would be Cheviot sheep. (translator's note)

37 This is a literal translation of the Gaelic; the equivalent Canadian term would be "underbrush."

38 Whiskey.

39 Leek.

40 MacDougall uses the Gaelic "sgian-dubh," a short-bladed, black-hilted sheath-knife or dagger, more commonly worn in the stocking as part of Highland dress. The literal translation is "black-dagger."

41 Falkirk tryst. (translator's note)

42 MacDougall is punning here — something which is lost in the English translation. The Gaelic "bochduinn" means "poverty," but also "bad luck" or "mischief." Thus, impoverished emigrants are likely to create mischief.

43 The original spelling and punctuation have been kept, even when it seems an error has been made by MacDougall. Robert MacDougall ultimately settled in Australia.

44 Spelling and puncuation have been left as in the original, even when it seems likely a mistake has been made.

45 Spelling, punctuation, and biographical details have been kept as in the original, even when it seems likely a mistake has been made.

Translator's Note: Facal
on Eadar-Theangair

This translation of Robert MacDougall's *Ceann-iuil an Fhir-imrich do dh'America mu-Thuath* endeavors to provide a modern English version of a Scots Gaelic text, respecting the cadence and tenor of the original. Something, however, is always lost in translation, most importantly the nuances of meaning introduced when the author chooses one word over another, or expresses one concept using varying synonymous terms – these can only be appreciated in the original language.

The Gaelic of this text is honest, heartfelt and shows Rob MacDhughaill's inextricable links to his culture, language and homeland. Gaelic culture is one of story, poetry and song, and MacDougall relates to his reader by ably drawing from these resources. As the *sgeulaiche* (storyteller), the author presents information to the emigrant by means of exemplary anecdotes throughout the text. Accompanying this illustrative prose is a large store of Gaelic *sean-fhaclan* (proverbs). Known to all who read the book, these wise sayings are part of the everyday speech patterns of the language. Also dear to this well-read writer are the great bards of seventeenth-(Mairi Nighean Alasdair Ruaidh, Murchadh Mor mac mhic Mhurchaidh, An Ciaran Mabach), eighteenth-(Donnchadh Ban Mac an t-Saoir, Alasdair Mac Mhaighstir Alasdair) and early nineteenth-century (Eoghan MacLachlainn) Gaelic poetry, from whom he frequently quotes or paraphrases. Of these, nature and praise poetry serve the author's purpose well (particularly Duncan Ban Macintyre's "*Moladh Beinn Dobhrain*"), as he describes a land of wilderness, farms and unique individuals. As a man of strong Christian faith, he had a thorough knowledge of his Gaelic Scriptures and quotes often from them. The translation of these passages conforms to the words of the Gaelic Bible, but bears similarities to the

English of the Authorized Version and the New International Version. Religious poetry, particularly that of another Gaelic-speaking emigrant and kinsman from Perthshire, Rev. James MacGregor, plays an important role in the text, affirming MacDougall's own assertions and exhortations concerning lifestyle in the new land.

MacDougall was intrigued by similarities he perceived between the Highland Gael and the native peoples of North America. Though his imaginative musings about a common cultural and linguistic heritage are unsound, they depict a great admiration for and sense of kinship with the original inhabitants of the emigrants' new world. Even today, the reader can share MacDougall's sense of awe when he encountered Algonquin terms such as *Saganash* (white man) and *moccasin* (footwear), comparing them to his own *Sasannach* (English) and *mu chasan* (around the feet). MacDougall may have inspired the later words of Duncan Black Blair's poem on Niagara Falls (*"Eas Niagara"*) when he likened the sound and meaning of Niagara to his own *Gaelic Abhainn* <u>*na Gairich*</u> (<u>the roaring</u> river), again suggesting to him a common bond between the Gaels and aboriginal North Americans.

The Gaels themselves described Canada at times as *An Talamh Fhuar* (the cold land) or *Tir nan Craobh* (land of the trees). MacDougall, like all Gaels, had a great love of his language, but the culture of the new world appeared to have little use for Gaelic, the first language of many thousands of Scottish immigrants to Canada. Although Gaelic survived well into the twentieth century in Bruce and Glengarry counties, this vividly descriptive language has ceased to remain a part of the daily life of native-born Ontarians of Scottish heritage. Its legacy, however, is to be found throughout the province in its history and place names. We hope that this English translation of Robert MacDougall's Guide will bring to a new readership the words and thoughts of a Scottish Gael who sojourned for a time in Tir nan Craobh.

DAVID LIVINGSTON-LOWE

Bibliography

Aldwinckle, Mary, and R.E. Thompson. "McDougall/ MacDougall." *Goderich Township Families*, 1985. Ed. Alison Lobb. Goderich Township: Private Publication, 1985. 197-200.

Aliquis. *Observations on the History and Recent Proceedings of the Canada Company; Addressed in Four Letters to Frederick Widder, Esq., One of the Commissioners.* 1845.

Armstrong, F.H., et al., eds. *Aspects of Nineteenth-Century Ontario: Essays Presented to James J. Talman.* Toronto: U of Toronto P, 1974.

Bell, Rev. William. *Hints to Emigrants; in a Series of Letters From Upper Canada.* Edinburgh: Waugh and Innes, 1824.

Blackie, John Stuart. *The Language and Literature of the Scottish Highlands.* Edinburgh: Edmonston and Douglas, 1876.

Boulton, D'Arcy. *Sketch of His Majesty's Province of Upper Canada.* 1805. Toronto: Baxter, 1961.

Cage, R.A., ed. *The Scots Abroad: Labour, Capital, Enterprise, 1750-1914.* London: Croom Helm, 1985.

Cameron, Rev. Alexander. *Reliquiae Celticae, Texts, Papers, and Studies in Gaelic Literature and Philology left by the late Alexander Cameron, L.L.D.* Ed. Alexander MacBain, M.A., and Rev. John Kennedy. Inverness: Northern Chronicle, 1892.

Cameron, James M. "A Study of the Factors that Assisted and Directed Scottish Emigration to Upper Canada, 1815-1855." Diss. U of Glasgow, 1970.

Campbell, Duncan. *The Book of Garth and Fortingall: Historical Sketches Relating to the Districts of Garth, Fortingall, Athole, and Breadalbane.* Inverness: The Northern Counties Newspaper and Printing and Publishing Company, 1888.

Campbell, Duncan. *Reminiscences and Reflections of an Octogenarian Highlander.* Inverness: The Northern Counties Newspaper and Printing and Publishing Company, 1910.

Campbell, John Lorne. *Gaelic in Scottish Education and Life, Past, Present and Future.* Edinburgh: W. & A.K. Johnston, 1945.

Carrothers, W.A. *Emigration From the British Isles, With Special Reference to the Development of the Overseas Dominions.* London: P.S. King, 1929.

Cattermole, William. *Emigration. The Advantages of Emigration to Canada, Being the Substance of Two Lectures, Delivered at the Town-Hall, Colchester, and the Mechanics' Institution, Ipswich, by William Cattermole.* Coles Canadiana Collection. 1831. Toronto: Coles, 1970.

Clark, Neil. *A Letter From Canada*. Glasgow: N. Campbell, 1860.

Coleman, Thelma. *The Canada Company*. Stratford: County of Perth and Cumming Publishers, 1978.

Cowan, Helen. *British Emigration to British North America: The First Hundred Years*. Toronto: U of Toronto P, 1961.

Devine, T.M., ed. *Scottish Emigration and Scottish Society: Proceedings of the Scottish Historical Studies Seminar, University of Strathclyde, 1990-91*. Edinburgh: John Donald, 1992.

Donaldson, Gordon. *The Scots Overseas*. London: Robert Hale, 1966.

Doyle, Martin. *Hints on Emigration to Canada; Especially Addressed to the Lower Classes in Great Britain and Ireland*. Edinburgh: Oliver and Boyd, 1831.

Dunlop, William. *Tiger Dunlop's Upper Canada*. Introd. Carl F. Klinck. NCL 55. Ed. Malcolm Ross. Toronto: McClelland and Stewart, 1967.

Dunn, Charles. "Check-list of Scottish Gaelic Writings in North America." *Irisleabhar Ceilteach*. 1-2 (1952-1954): 23-29.

Dunn, Charles. *Highland Settler: A Portrait of the Scottish Gael in Nova Scotia*. Toronto: U of Toronto P, 1953.

Ellis, M.H. *The Beef Shorthorn in Australia*. Melbourne: Sidney and Melbourne Publishing Company, 1932.

Evans, Francis A. *The Emigrant's Directory and Guide to Obtain Lands and Effect a Settlement in the Canadas*. Edinburgh: Oliver and Boyd, 1833.

Fraser, Joshua. *Shanty, Forest and River Life in the Backwoods of Canada*. Montreal: John Lovell, 1883.

Galt, John. *Bogle Corbet*. Introd. Elizabeth Waterston. NCL 135. Ed. Malcolm Ross. Toronto: McClelland and Stewart, 1977.

Geike, John C. *Life in the Woods: A Boy's Narrative of the Adventures of a Settler's Family in Canada*. Boston: Crosby and Ainsworth, 1865.

Gourlay, Robert. *General Introduction to a Statistical Account of Upper Canada, Compiled with a view to a Grand System of Emigration, In Connection with a Reform of the Poor Law*. 1822. New York: Johnson Reprint Corporation, 1966.

Guillet, Edwin C. *Early Life in Upper Canada*. Toronto: U of Toronto P, 1933.

Guillet, Edwin C. *The Great Migration: The Atlantic Crossing by Sailing Ship Since 1770*. Toronto: U of Toronto P, 1937.

Guillet, Edwin C. *The Pioneer Farmer and Backwoodsman*. 2 vols. Toronto: Ontario

Publishing Co., 1963.

Harper, Marjory. "Image and Reality in Early Emigrant Literature." *British Journal of Canadian Studies* 7.1 (1992): 3-14.

Hildebrandt, Ruth Nancy. "Migration and Economic Change in the Northern Highlands During the Nineteenth Century, With Particular Reference to the Period 1851-1891." Diss. U of Glasgow, 1980.

Hill, Douglas. *The Scots to Canada.* Great Emigrations. Ed. Douglas Hill. London: Gentry Books, 1972.

Howison, John. *Sketches of Upper Canada, Domestic, Local, and Characteristic: To Which are Added, Practical Details for the Information of Emigrants of Every Class; and Some Recollections of the United States of America.* Edinburgh: Oliver and Boyd, 1821.

Hunt, Thornton Leigh. *Canada and South Australia. A Commentary on that part of the Earl of Durham's Report which relates to the Disposal of Waste Lands and Emigration. In Three Papers, Delivered at the South Australian Rooms, No. 5 Adam Street, Strand.* London: A. Gole, 1839.

Jackson, H.J.M. *British Emigration Policy, 1815-1830: "Shovelling out Paupers."* Oxford: Clarendon, 1972.

Jackson, John Mills. *A View of the Political Situation of the Province of Upper Canada, in North America. In Which her Physical Capacity is Stated; The Means of Diminishing her Burden, Encreasing her Value, and Securing her Connection to Great Britain, are fully considered. With Notes and Appendix.* London: W. Earle, 1809.

Jameson, Anna. *Winter Studies and Summer Rambles in Canada.* 3 vols. Coles Canadiana Collection. 1838. Toronto: Coles, 1972.

Johnson, J.K., and Bruce G. Wilson, eds. *Historical Essays on Upper Canada: New Perspectives.* Carleton Library Series 146. Ottawa: Carleton UP, 1989.

Johnston, Hugh. "Stratford and Goderich in the Days of the Canada Company." *Ontario History* 63.2 (1971): 71-86.

Jones, Dallas L. "The Background and Motives of Scottish Emigration to the United States of America in the Period 1815-1861, With Special Reference to Emigrant Correspondence." Diss. U of Edinburgh, 1970.

Kelly, Kenneth. "The Evaluation of Land for Wheat Cultivation in Early Nineteenth Century Ontario." *Ontario History* 62.1 (1970): 57-64.

Kerrigan, Catherine, ed. *The Immigrant Experience: Proceedings of a Conference Held at the University of Guelph, 8-11 June 1989.* Guelph: U of Guelph, 1992.

Kiddle, Margaret. *Men of Yesterday: A Social History of the Western District of Victoria, 1834-1890.* Melbourne: Melbourne UP, 1963.

Knight, Charles. *One Hundred and Fifty Wood Cuts, Selected from The Penny Magazine; Worked, by the Printing-Machine, From the Original Blocks.* London: Charles Knight, 1835.

Lamond, Robert. *A Narrative of the Rise and Progress of Emigration, From the Counties of Lanark and Renfrew, to the New Settlements in Upper Canada, on Government Grant; Comprising the Proceedings of the Glasgow Committee for Directing the Affairs and Embarkation of the Societies. With a Map of the Townships, Designs for Cottages, and a Plan of the Ship Earl of Buckinghamshire. Also, Interesting Letters from the Settlements.* Glasgow: Chalmers and Collins, 1821.

"The Late Mr. Robert McDougall." *The Age,* Melbourne. 29 June 1887.

Lizars, Robina, and Kathleen MacFarlane Lizars. *In the Days of the Canada Company: The Story of the Settlement of the Huron Tract and a View of the Social Life of the Period.* Introd. G.M. Grant. Coles Canadiana Collection. 1896. Toronto: Coles, 1972.

Lobb, Alison, ed. *The Township of Goderich History.* Township of Goderich: Township of Goderich, 1984.

MacDonald, Rev. Angus. *The MacDonald Collection of Gaelic Poetry.* Inverness: The Northern Counties Newspaper and Printing and Publishing, 1911.

MacDonell, Margaret. *The Emigrant Experience: Songs of Highland Emigrants in North America.* Toronto: U of Toronto P, 1982.

MacDougall, Robert. Diary of a voyage from England to Port Phillip, 1 Jan - 14 Feb 1842. Reel 2778. State Library of New South Wales, Sidney.

McGregor, John. *British America.* 2 vols. Edinburgh: William Blackwood, 1832.

MacKinnon, Kenneth. *Gaelic - A Past and Future Prospect.* Edinburgh: Saltire Society, 1991.

MacLean, Rev. Donald. *The Literature of the Scottish Gael.* Edinburgh: William Hodge, 1912.

MacLean, Rev. Donald. *Typographia Scoto-gadelica, or Books Printed in the Gaelic of Scotland from the Year 1567 to the Year 1914, With Bibliographical and Biographical Notes.* Edinburgh: John Grant, 1915.

MacLeod, Rev. Donald. *Memoir of Norman MacLeod, D.D.* New York: Charles Scribner, 1876.

MacLeod, Rev. Dr. Norman. *A Dictionary of the Gaelic Language. In Two Parts.* 4 vols. London: Henry G. Bohn, 1830.

MacLeod, Norman. "The Emigrant Ship." *Reminiscences of a Highland Parish.* 2nd Ed. London: 1833. 378-92.

MacNeill, Nigel, L.L.D. *The Literature of the Highlanders: Race, Language, Literature, Poetry and Music.* Ed. John MacMaster Campbell. 1892; rpt. Stirling: Eneas MacKay, 1929.

Magrath, Thomas. *Authentic Letters From Upper Canada; With an Account of Canadian Field Sports.* Ed. Rev. Thomas Radcliffe. Introd. James J. Talman. 1833; rpt. Toronto: Macmillan, 1953.

Mathison, John. *Counsel for Emigrants, and Interesting Information from Numerous Sources Concerning British America, The United States, and New South Wales, &c., &c.* 3rd edition. Aberdeen: John Mathison, 1838.

Mitchell, Dugald, M.D., ed. *The Book of Highland Verse: An (English) Anthology Consisting of (a) Translations from Gaelic (b) English Verse relating to the Highlands.* Paisley: Alexander Gardner, 1912.

Moodie, Susanna. *Roughing It in the Bush; or, Life in Canada.* Ed. Elizabeth Thompson. 1852. Ottawa: Tecumseh, 1997.

Peck, Harry H. *Memoirs of a Stockman.* 1942. Melbourne: Stockland P, 1946.

Quaife, G.R. "Robert McDougall (1813-1887)." *Australian Dictionary of Biography.* Vol. 5. Ed. Bede Nairn, Geoffrey Serle, and Russel Ward. Melbourne: Melbourne UP, 1974.

Reid, W. Stanford, ed. *The Scottish Tradition in Canada.* Toronto: McClelland and Stewart, 1976.

Review of *Emigrant's Guide to North America. Cuairtear nan Gleann* Sept. 1841: 205.

Rolph, Thomas. *Canada v. Australia: Their Comparative Merits Considered in an Answer to a Pamphlet, by Thornton Leigh Hunt, Esq. Entitled "Canada and Australia."* London: Smith, Elder, 1839.

Rolph, Thomas. *Comparative Advantages Between the United States and Canada.* London: Smith, Elder, 1842.

Rolph, Thomas. *A Descriptive and Statistical Account of Canada.* 2nd ed. London: Smith, Elder, 1841.

Rolph, Thomas. *Emigration and Colonization.* London: J. Mortimer, 1844. Scott, James. *Huron County in Pioneer Times.* Seaforth: Huron County Historical Committee, 1954.

Shaw, J. "Brief Beginnings: Nova Scotian and Old World Bards Compared." *Scottish Gaelic Studies* 10 (1965): 342-355.

Shirreff, Patrick. *A Tour Through North America; Together with a comprehensive view of the Canadas and United States. As Adapted for Agricultural Emigration.* Edinburgh:

Oliver and Boyd, 1835.

Sinclair, Sir John. *Specimen of the Statistical Account of Scotland. Drawn up from the communications of the ministers of the different parishes.* Edinburgh: np, 1791.

Smith, W.L. *The Pioneers of Old Ontario.* Toronto: George N. Morang, 1923.

Smythe, David William. *A Short Topographical Description of His Majesty's Province of Upper Canada, in North America. To Which is Annexed a Provincial Gazetteer.* London: W. Faden, 1799.

Stewart, Major-General David. *Sketches of the Character, Manners, and Present State of the Highlanders of Scotland; with Details of the Military Service of the Highland Regiments.* 3rd ed. Vol. 1. Edinburgh: Archibald Constable, 1825.

Strickland, Samuel. *Twenty-Seven Years in Canada West; or, the Experience of an Early Settler.* Ed. Agnes Strickland. 2 vols. London: Richard Bentley, 1853.

Thompson, Elizabeth. *The Pioneer Woman: A Canadian Character Type.* Montreal: McGill-Queen's UP, 1991.

Thompson Family Papers. Clinton, Ontario.

Traill, Catharine Parr. *The Backwoods of Canada: Being Letters from the Wife of an Emigrant Officer, Illustrative of the Domestic Economy of British America.* Afterword D.M.R. Bentley. NCL. Ed. David Staines. 1836. Toronto: McClelland and Stewart, 1989.

The Victorian Agricultural and Horticultural Gazette 1.1 (1857): 5-6; 1.8 (1857): 87-90; 1.12 (1858): 145-6; 2.13 (1858): 9; 2.16 (1858): 46-7; 2.17 (1858): 61; 2.19 (1858): 91; 2.20 (1858): 99-101, 105-6.

Walker, Dr. John. *The Rev. Dr. John Walker's Report on the Hebrides of 1764 and 1771.* Ed. Margaret M. McKay. Edinburgh: John Donald, 1980.

Watson, William J., ed. *Rosg Gaidhlig: Specimens of Gaelic Prose.* 2nd ed. Glasgow: Alex MacLaren, 1929.

Willis, N.P., Esq. *Canadian Scenery, Illustrated in a series of Views by W. H. Bartlett.* 2 vols. London: George Virtue, 1848.

Withers, Charles W.J. *Gaelic in Scotland, 1698-1981: The Geographical History of a Language.* Foreward. Derick S. Thomson. Edinburgh: John Donald, 1984.

Index

About The Editor

ELIZABETH THOMPSON is a writer living in Toronto, Ontario. She has taught at the University of Toronto and The University of Western Ontario. She has written extensively about early Canadian literature, as well as contemporary Canadian fiction and poetry. Her publications include *The Pioneer Woman: A Canadian Character Type* (1991) and an edition of Susanna Moodie's *Roughing It in the Bush* (1997). As a direct descendant of the MacDougalls, she is happy to introduce a wider audience to her family.

Depending on the source, the spelling of the author's surname varies between MacDougall and McDougall. The use of MacDougall (the varient which appears in critical and historical references to the book) is used throughout this text to ensure consistency.